FASTING
THAT MOVES
GOD'S HAND

T. L. LOWERY

T.L. LOWER
GLOBAL FOUNDA

FASTING That Moves God's Hand
Dr. T. L. Lowery
T.L. Lowery Ministries, International
P.O. Box 2440
Cleveland, Tennessee 37320-2550

ISBN: 978-1-59684-591-6
Library of Congress Control Number: 2011929831

Endorsements

It's not only exciting, but refreshing, to pick up a book about a subject that was not just written from a moment of inspiration after reading the Bible, but was penned by the hand of a person who has personally experienced what he has written. During my many years of ministry, I have never known one man who has spent more time in fasting, than Dr. T.L. Lowery.

As an eleven year old sitting in the open aired tabernacle in Roanoke, Virginia, I saw the first dramatic miracle occur under T.L. Lowery's ministry, when he prayed for a man unable to walk without a cane, and I saw the power of God overcome the fellow and he began running, unaided at full speed around the tabernacle. It was also then that I felt the Presence of the Holy Spirit for the first time.

When I was about 19 years old, I saw Dr. Lowery on the 40th day of an extended fast, holding on to the pulpit from being physically weak, attempting to preach a message at the Church of God Camp meeting in Birmingham, Alabama. Within moments, he was transformed from a weak vessel, to a man on fire for God! Suddenly, the Glory of God fell upon over 4,000 people and that night a demon possessed girl was delivered and set free, as hundreds streamed to the altar for deliverance, healing and salvation.

From the very beginning, the ministry of T.L. Lowery was marked by the miraculous. As a traveling evangelist, when men and women heard T.L. was coming to preach, there was a high level of expectancy hovering over the congregation as they knew, "God's man of faith and power," was about to bring the Word and through the Holy Spirit, demonstrate the Gospel through signs and wonders. The secret among those who knew him best was he lived a life of fasting and consecration to God.

After many, many years of ministry, he was again on an extended fast, when he was asked by a fellow minister, "Why are you fasting – again"? Dr. Lowery replied, "There is a place in God that I haven't found yet, and I want to seek Him till I can find it!" Such hunger must be replicated in this next generation.

If you desire a closer walk with God, a spiritual breakthrough, a miracle of answered prayer, then fasting holds the key to the impossible. Take a lesson and spiritual advice from a man who not only knows what the Bible, church history and church tradition teaches about fasting, but has put the practice in operation throughout his ministry. It is time to learn the art of fasting and repeat this powerful practice, to break the yokes that are binding men! This book is the manual for those who desire a closer walk with God through fasting!

A Spiritual Son of T.L. Lowery
Perry Stone, Jr.

We are living in a tumultuous time when it is unequivocally imperative that the Church in America return to its pure, Divinely-birthed Apostolic roots, heritage, and state of being – days that hark back to the incomparable early days of the Church that Jesus Himself set up on earth for His Father, days that evoke, preserve, recreate, and propagate the concentrated intensity of anointing, power, and consecration that thrived in the holiness and Pentecostal movements of our nation's previous century.

The only way for this to take place is for the Church to embrace and fully receive the true Apostolic Message, Movement, and Ministry that began with the early apostles, and which will, among many other things, unearth and re-establish many bedrock foundational principles and mysteries of the Kingdom that have fallen out of vogue with today's Christianity and society.

One such core tenet is the eternal importance of fasting; and I personally know no other man of God who has lived and exemplified this principle, as well as has reaped its priceless spiritual benefits, more than Dr. T.L. Lowery, a spectacular, iconic, yet always humble servant of God, and my spiritual father in the anointing.

Over the nearly 40 years that I have known and served in the Gospel with Dr. T.L. Lowery, I have witnessed him undergo numerous fasts – 40-

day fasts, 30-day fasts, 21-day fasts, and many more. I personally spoke with Dr. Lowery on a daily and then weekly basis during one such 40-day fast in 1982, at the end of which God spoke to him to go to Washington, DC, and begin the work that would become the National Church of God.

Prayer and fasting have been an essential earmark and backbone of Dr. Lowery's personal and ministry life; he has told me himself that it was necessary for him to consistently fast in order to maintain the high level of the powerful, penetrating, fiery anointing that God has poured out upon him and with which He has entrusted him. All who know Dr. Lowery would wholeheartedly agree that his dedication and conscientiousness in prayer and fasting have borne their fruit in his life abundantly, for this inimitable anointing still rests generously upon and within Dr. Lowery, his effectiveness and determination in furthering the Gospel forges ahead unwaveringly, and his entire life and ministry are characterized by the eternally impacting touch and transformation of the LORD.

King David said, "…I humbled my soul with fasting, and my prayer returned into mine own bosom." (Psalm 35:13) Fasting, which keeps one's soul in keen, subjected relationship to the Spirit of God, which fosters deep, abiding humility before the LORD, which helps to regenerate and reactivate a passionate, vehement, continual craving and pursuit of God, and which is instrumental in facilitating the Holy Ghost to purify the stale, languishing Church, to convict and bring to repentance the lost, and to sweep a nation with the blazing fires of holy, enduring revival, is a foundational precept of the LORD that must be reinstated into today's – and tomorrow's – era of Christianity.

Dr. T.L. Lowery has truly become an incarnate epistle of this principle, and can well instruct every one of us in this matter. May this book have its Divinely intended result in the lives and ministries of all who read it!

Dr. H.B. Seymour
The Father's House International
Westminster, SC

Fasting That Moves the Hand of God might well be Dr. T.L. Lowery's best book ever. It is scripturally sound, historically factual, and personally illustrated. Fasting has always been a lifestyle to Dr. Lowery. This publication teaches us how to make it our lifestyle too . . . and what can happen when we do.

Dr. Raymond F. Culpepper
General Overseer Church of God International

I have known Dr. Lowery for many years and encourage you to read his new book. He has devoted his life to furthering the kingdom of God. Fasting is a very important spiritual discipline and this book will help you greatly in understanding the benefits. I personally fast many days every year along with our church members and have heard miraculous testimonies as a result of seeking God through fasting.

Dr. Bob Rodgers
Senior Pastor
Evangel World Prayer Center
Louisville, KY

"The Bible says in the last days men will be lovers of pleasures more than lovers of God. We are surely living in the last days, because our society has become self-absorbed and self-obsessed.

Even in the midst of gross darkness, I believe that a mighty move of Pentecostal power has begun among God's people, and that we are about to see a great outpouring of signs and wonders. This revival will continue on the wings of disciplines such as fasting and fervent prayer.

Dr. T. L. Lowery, one of the last great generals of the faith, has provided a guide book for the days ahead. He is as qualified as any man alive to point the way to return to God with fasting and genuine faith."

Mrs. Ellen Parsley
World Harvest Church

We call those who can see further and more clearly than others visionaries. We call those who tell the truth when others cringe in craven silence courageous. We call those who survey the scene of battle and are unafraid to move forward leaders. We call those who have been through the fire and stand steadfast tried and tested. Dr. T. L. Lowery is all these and more.

In his new book, Dr. Lowery reintroduces us to a long-neglected and much misunderstood discipline of the church that was employed to great effect in ages past—fasting. Unfortunately, fasting has fallen out of favor and is considered a quaint oddity in our modern, high-speed, high-tech, chromium plated set of religious exercises we call 21st century Christianity. The church's present powerlessness is adequate testimony of the consequences of our neglect.

The fasting to which God calls us, and of which Dr. Lowery faithfully reminds us, is neither the extreme asceticism of the ancient hermit nor the gimmickry of the modern showman. It is instead the legitimate expression of a heart fully consumed with seeking God in genuine humility and forthright repentance.

There is much to be gained in a return to the discarded values of the past. I know of no more reliable guide than Dr. T. L. Lowery.

Rod Parsley
World Harvest Church

Dedication

I would like to dedicate this book to
my wonderful wife, Mildred who has
faithfully stood at my side for 63 years.
Her commitment and dedication to prayer
and fasting through the years has been
a tremendous strength to me personally
as well as to many thousands in the nations
where we have ministered.

When great men are remembered, it is often in terms of what they did. It might be a more fair assessment to speak of the results of what they did. Many preachers, for example, may be recognized as outstanding orators; however, a reasonable question to ask might be, "What happened as the result of their preaching?"

When history evaluates Thomas Lanier Lowery, a great many positive and complimentary statements are certain to be written about his ministry. He will be honored as an outstanding pastor who dedicated his ministry to two congregations: North Cleveland in Tennessee and National in Washington, D.C. But he didn't just "pastor"; he brought in a harvest of souls, he grew churches exponentially, he built impressive facilities, he established a model Bible school, he served his cities with caring ministries and outreaches.

He will be recognized as a distinguished and world-renowned evangelist. But he didn't just hold meetings; he conducted citywide and regional crusades, filled giant stadiums, crisscrossed the nation with a 10,000-seat tent cathedral, traveled to 115 countries around the globe. In the process, only heaven knows the hundreds and thousands of people redeemed, Spirit-filled, healed, delivered, and added to the Kingdom. Hundreds followed him into gospel ministry as he challenged them with the calling of God.

T.L. Lowery will be lionized as a visionary church executive who served in the top tier of denominational leadership for the Church of God for 32 years, half that time as a member of the International Executive Committee, a tenure almost unequaled. But he did not just sit at a desk; he set goals, challenged fellow leaders to greater vision, modeled servant leadership, headed action committees, inspired those he led.

Then, at the age when most people retire to sit on the porch and rock, T.L. Lowery did not retire—he "refired." He launched the T.L. Lowery Global Foundation, which became the crown jewel of his nearly seven decades of ministry. He established a training center in Cleveland, Tennessee, where the next generation of God-called men and women gather periodically to learn from Dr. Lowery and other generals of the faith the "how-to" of a power-filled and anointed outworking of ministry. Like all of his previous ministerial assignments, this one, too, is having world-impacting results.

One of his strong training emphases has been on the foundation stones of successful ministry: prayer and fasting. That has inspired this book, to which I commend your attention.

Fasting might rightly be denominated "The Forgotten Practice" of Christianity in the twenty-first century. A regular feature of New Testament faith life, fasting was practiced in the early centuries of the church; however, as the church lost its vital life connection with its Founder, and the Holy Spirit's ministry was consigned to the dustbin of history, fasting became abused by ascetics who starved themselves without spiritual benefit. Long periods of fanatical asceticism likely led to the pendular reaction that has denied the benefits of fasting to generations of believers.

Dr. Lowery, in *Fasting That Moves God's Hand*, describes the biblical grounding of fasting, outlines its advantages, and encourages its practice.

Like all of his previous expressions of ministry, the production of this book is sure to have outstanding results. Happily, the results will accrue to the Kingdom, and to you, personally, who follow his counsel.

Bill George
Secretary
T.L. Lowery Global Foundation

Table of Contents

The practice of fasting within the Church today has greatly diminished through the years and its spiritual significance as an important Christian discipline as almost disappeared. Yet, there has never been another time in the history of the Church that it is more needed!

Prayer and fasting enables us to move the hand of God! This is the hour God wants to unleash the 'atomic bomb' of fasting within the Church to enable us to fulfill His will in reaching and winning the lost in our cities and nations.

Fasting as a mere act of abstaining from food in self denial or as a form of spiritual discipline does not produce spiritual breakthrough. The fasting that God honors and moves His hand on our behalf and on behalf of nations is the fast that begins with the attitude of the heart.

Too often in the Church we concentrate on the method or strategies used in fasting and give very little thought concerning our motives and the attitudes of our hearts. We cannot expect our fasting to move God's hand if our hearts are not right before Him and if we are not living in accordance with His Word.

The importance of Biblical fasting in the life of every true disciple of Jesus Christ cannot be overemphasized. As we look closely at Jesus' teaching, you will clearly see that it is not a matter of "If" you should fast, but rather, "When" you fast.

God has given the Church the awesome responsibility and privilege through prayer and fasting to move His hand on behalf of our families, cities and nations. It is not a matter of can we do it, but will we?

INTRODUCTION

We have received a sovereign commission and have been given divine power and authority through Christ to set our cities and nations free from satan's bondage. And while the Church has experienced tremendous growth and has made dynamic advances in recent years into seemingly impenetrable areas once considered "closed" to the Gospel, it is not operating in the fullness of power Christ intended.

This is the hour God's power will be seen in the Church of Jesus Christ as never before!

However, before the Church can experience the fullness of God's power in the extent He has ordained for this hour, we must be willing to:

- Hear His voice
- Be led by His Spirit
- Pay the price

We must first hear the call of the Spirit to fast and pray, then He will release His apostolic anointing upon us through a flood of His glory and bring in a harvest of souls such as the world has never seen!

This is not just a book on the subject of fasting to be read and placed on a book shelf somewhere to gather dust.

It is not just another call to set aside a specific amount of time to fast and when the fast is over continue on with business as usual.

My goal and purpose is to challenge you to answer the call of the Spirit and incorporate fasting as part of your lifestyle.

Sanctify a Fast!

With all my heart I believe the Father is calling me... He is calling you…to sanctify a fast. By His Spirit, God is calling His people to "Blow the trumpet in Zion, sanctify a fast, call a solemn assembly" (Joel 2:15).

The Hebrew word for sanctify is Qadash which means "to set apart as sacred, to observe as holy." True Biblical fasting is not an exercise of the natural man. It originates in the spirit and is an attitude of the heart. When we sanctify a fast we shut out the things of the world around us and set ourselves apart to draw near to God.

When Daniel understood, through reading the

prophecies of Jeremiah, that the captivity of the children of Israel would be completed in 70 years, he sanctified a fast—he set himself apart through fasting and prayer. He said, "I set my face unto the Lord God, to seek by prayer and supplications, with fasting, and sackcloth and ashes" (Daniel 9:3).

Daniel set his face to seek the Lord with prayer and with fasting. In other words, he set himself apart with the one goal of seeking God. I believe he determined to stay in an attitude of fasting and prayer until he heard from God. He humbled himself, confessed his sins and the sins of the people and poured out his heart in deep intercession. From the moment he humbled himself in fasting and prayer, God dispatched an angel—Gabriel—with the revelation he needed.

Fasting for an Endtime Global Spiritual Awakening

I am issuing a call to pastors, Christian leaders and believers everywhere to unite with me in seasons of corporate and individual fasts, believing God for a global spiritual awakening and an unprecedented outpouring of God's Spirit resulting in city and nation-wide transformation.

I believe this is an end-time call of the Spirit to bring in a great, final harvest of souls before Christ's return. He that has ears to hear, let him hear what the Spirit is saying to the Church!

I appreciate the various prayer and fasting initiatives around the world that have been launched in recent years. They have been powerful and have brought awareness to the power of prayer and fasting to change cities and nations. I believe they are the beginning of a sovereign move of God calling the Church to a new time and season of united global prayer and fasting that will result in unprecedented changes:

- in the political arena,

- in the alignment of nations,

- in the world's economies,

- in the expansion of God's Kingdom into the remote unreached areas of the world

The scale and dimension of prayer and fasting I believe He is calling the Church to now is much more far reaching in scope and intensity than anything we have yet experienced. The time has come when the Church must unite globally, lay aside our denominational and doctrinal differences and agendas and release a resounding cry before God's Throne for a great end time outpouring of His Spirit.

What does it really mean to sanctify a fast?

What is the spiritual significance of fasting and what is its purpose?

Why is fasting important and why is it necessary to fast?

Throughout the pages of this book we will go in depth into the Scriptures to answer these questions and more.

As we do, the Father will reveal His heart.

You will understand why fasting is so important today and why it is a vital, powerful spiritual resource He wants to activate in your life.

The destiny of cities, nations, people groups and this world is at stake!

It is in the hands of those who will answer this call of the Spirit and submit themselves into the hands of God to be used, through prayer and fasting, to bring down His power and a move of His Spirit resulting in a worldwide harvest of souls.

Will you be one of those who hear and respond to this call of the Spirit?

FASTING

THAT MOVES GOD'S HAND

Chapter One

It's Time to Sanctify a Fast

"Blow the trumpet in Zion, sanctify a fast,
call a solemn assembly"
Joel 2:16

It's Time to Sanctify a Fast

Today the cry is coming forth from the heavens, "Blow the trumpet in Zion, sanctify a fast, call a solemn assembly" (Joel 2:15). In the midst of this crooked and perverse generation, God is calling His people to repentance. He is calling pastors, evangelists and Christian leaders to lead the people of God in seasons of fasting and prayer where they are confessing and forsaking sin that they have allowed to come into their midst. He is calling us first to humble ourselves in fasting and prayer—confessing and turning from our sins.

Look around you! Our cities and nations are spiritually desolate! Here in America, a war is raging for the sanctity of marriage and to stop those who want to redefine marriage and sanction homosexual marriages.

Millions of unborn babies have been murdered, abortion clinics flourish and promiscuity among teens is rampant. Men and women living together before marriage is no longer a disgrace or shame, but is considered normal!

> We face crises in almost every nation on earth and it seems we are set on a path of destruction that seems unstoppable.

Divorce, immorality, sexual perversion, pornography and adultery have infiltrated the Church. Prominent Christian leaders, who should be setting the example of a Godly lifestyle, have become involved in illicit affairs, sex scandals and are divorcing and remarrying without remorse. Instead of setting high moral standards, the Church continues to sanction this type of behavior and things which were once considered shameful are overlooked and swept under the carpet.

What is the Answer to the Crises We Face?

The problems and challenges we face currently in the Church, in America and in the nations cannot be met by man's ingenuity, abilities or natural wisdom.

We are living in the time of great perplexity Jesus

said would come upon the earth before His return. He said there would be wars and rumours of wars. *"For nation shall rise against nation, and kingdom against kingdom: and there shall be famines, and pestilences, and earthquakes, in divers places"* (Matthew 24:7). He said on earth there would be distress of nations, *"with perplexity: the sea and the waves roaring: Men's hearts failing them for fear, and for looking after those things which are coming on the earth..."* (Luke 21:25-26).

We face crises in almost every nation on earth and it seems we are set on a path of destruction that appears unstoppable. There are political and economic crises for which man has no answers. Just within the past few years we have seen thousands killed through the devastation of tsunamis, earthquakes, famines, floods and other catastrophic events. We face the threat of terrorist attacks and the possibility of a nuclear war. A full-scale war could erupt in the Middle East at any time as Iran continues to develop its nuclear program.

The economies of the world are crumbling and there seems to be no remedy. Multiplied thousands in the United States have lost their homes and unemployment has skyrocketed.

The powers and principalities of darkness have established strongholds and have gained a stranglehold on entire people groups. Multitudes are headed for eternal destruction in hell and yet the Church in North America and Europe has never been more ineffective in confronting the spiritual and moral decay that has infected Western civilization.

> God is raising up an army of intercessors who have made fasting and prayer a lifestyle. Will you answer the call?

While we have established large mega churches, with numerous sophisticated church programs, and have developed fine-tuned community ministry outreaches in an attempt to impact our cities, the Church for the most part has been unable to penetrate and dispel the spiritual darkness permeating our society.

America is at a Spiritual Crossroads!

America has sinned against God by not only turning away from Him, but we have rejected His laws and the godly moral standards based on His Word. We give evidence of being a post-Christian culture. Demonic strongholds of abortion, homosexuality, adultery, pornography, fornication, violence, greed and immorality have taken root.

Families are being destroyed through divorce. Children are no longer safe in the school yards or in their homes and must be protected from demon-possessed child molesters. Young people are no longer able to cope and are turning to drugs, crime and suicide.

When Christ ascended into Heaven, He made full provision that His Church would be the most powerful force on earth. He intended that it would carry on the same supernatural ministry He had—healing the sick, casting out devils, raising the dead and building the Kingdom of God on the earth. Yet, when faced with the current crises and problems in our communities, cities and nations, the Church is facing a power crisis!

The great need we are confronted with in the Church is not for more man-made programs, more massive buildings, more organization, more smooth tongued orators, more seminars and training tools in church growth. What we need is not more political activism or social outreach. And, believe it or not, our greatest need is not for more finances!

Our greatest need is for an outpouring of God's Spirit that will empower the Church, release a wave of salvation, healing and deliverance to the masses and bring transformation in our cities and nations! And this will only come as the result of the Church answering the global call to seasons of fasting and prayer.

We need those who will commit to more than just one-time fasting events.

God is raising up an army of intercessors who have made fasting and prayer a *lifestyle* and who are willing to pay the price on their knees for a global spiritual awakening and the promised outpouring in Joel 2:28.

Will you answer the call? Are you willing to pay the price?

Prayer, Fasting & Repentance are the Keys to Revival

As we look back through Church history, we see that every great move of God and major revival was ushered in through united prayer and fasting. Matthew Henry, Johnathan Edwards, David Brainerd, Charles Finney,

Charles H. Spurgeon, Andrew Murray, Rees Howell, John Hyde, William Seymour, Smith Wigglesworth and a host of other men and women who were greatly used by God to bring revival and great advances to the Kingdom of God, gave themselves to fasting and prayer.

> Prayer is the one hand with which we grasp the invisible; fasting the other with which we let loose and cast away the visible.
> Andrew Murray

John Wesley firmly believed in fasting and personally fasted every Wednesday and Friday. One of his requirements of those desiring to minister with him, evangelize or pastor a church founded through that movement was required to commit themselves to fast and pray every Wednesday and Friday. He once said,

And with fasting let us always join in fervent prayer, pouring out our whole souls before God, confessing our sins with all their aggravations, humbling ourselves under his mighty hand, laying open before him all our wants, all our guiltiness and helplessness. This is a season for enlarging our prayers, both in behalf of ourselves and of our brethren. Let us now bewail the sins of our people, and cry aloud for the city of our God: that the Lord may build up Zion, and cause his face to shine on her desolations. [1]

The prayers of John Welch were used by God to release a mighty outpouring of His Spirit upon Scotland. He prayed with such fervency and intensity on behalf of the lost he cried, "Give me Scotland, or I die." This is the type of prayer we must have today—fervent, passionate prayer that is set on fire by the Holy Spirit!

John Welch considered his day unproductive if he failed to spend eight to ten hours in prayer. In the night he would often get up to pray and his wife would complain when she found him lying on the floor weeping. He would tell her, "O woman, I have the souls of three thousand to answer for, and I know not how it is with many of them."

It is my prayer that God will ignite the fire of prayer, accompanied by seasons of fasting, in the heart of every person reading this book and that they will have this same passion and burden for souls.

The Great Awakening of 1857 Ushered in Through Prayer

During the Great Awakening in the United States in 1857, in one year more than one million people were saved. The Great Awakening is also referred to as The Prayer Revival because it was born and sustained through fasting and prayer. This move of God was not led by a great, well-known pastor or Christian leader, but by a layman who was desperately hungry for a move of God.

Jeremiah Lanphier, a businessman, opened the doors of the North Dutch Reformed Church in New York beginning a daily noon prayer meeting. People began to respond and they started meeting every day filling every public building in downtown New York. The news of the prayer meeting spread to outlying cities and other prayer groups sprang up.

After six months, 10,000 businessmen were meeting daily at noon in New York City alone! In eight months, from September until May, 50,000 people in New York City were saved. The move of God spread throughout New England where people met to pray three times a day. The revival spread up the Hudson River and down the Mohawk.

The fire spread from New York to other cities and then swept over the entire country.

Our whole nation was shaken by God's power as it had never been shaken before. The revival crossed the Atlantic, broke out in Northern Ireland, Scotland, Wales, England, South Africa and Southern India. In Northern Ireland four men met together every Saturday night to pray for revival. They spent the whole night in prayer. God heard their prayers and revival began to spread across Ireland. God's power was so strong in some parts of Ireland that courts adjourned because there were no cases to try. Jails were closed because there were no prisoners to incarcerate.

The Great Welsh Revival of 1904-05 Born Through Prayer and Fasting!

In the well-known revival that swept through Wales in 1904-05 more than 100,000 Welsh came to Christ. Men stopped gambling and drinking, bars were closed and casinos lost their customers. The political leaders from the Parliament in London abandoned themselves to the revival meetings and denominational barriers were broken down as believers and pastors experienced the awesome presence of God.

This mighty outpouring of God's Spirit came as a result of fasting and prayer. Evan Roberts, who was used to lead this revival, fasted and prayed for ten to eleven years before God moved His hand over Wales and the great Welsh revival took place. Because of his intense hunger for the Lord, Evan gave himself to fasting, prayer and intercession.

> There has never been another time in the history of the Church when the practice of true Biblical fasting has been more needed!

When Evan was twenty-one years old, he would awaken every night at 1:00 a.m. where he would be "taken up into divine fellowship" and would pray until 5:00 a.m. when he would fall back asleep before waking again at 9:00 a.m. continuing in prayer until noon. It has been said that Evan would break down, crying bitterly for God to "bend" the Church, in an agony of prayer with tears coursing down his cheeks and his whole body writhing.

Prayer & Fasting and the Great Azusa Street Revival that Swept Around the World!

William Seymour and Frank Bartleman fasted and prayed for almost seven years before the Azusa Street Revival broke out in 1906. The after-shock waves of this great outpouring of God's Spirit have been felt throughout the world for almost a century impacting almost every nation of the world. Today there are over 550 million Pentecostal and Charismatics who trace their spiritual heritage back to this awesome move of God!

For 250 Years Fast Days were Proclaimed Throughout America!

We know from American history that our forefathers practiced fasting and prayer as one of the essential spiritual disciplines of the Christian life. For more than 250 years (from 1600 until after the American Civil War) "fast days" were proclaimed by churches, denominations and government leaders.

In his book, "The Fast and Thanksgiving Days of

New England", Dr. DeLoss Love documents over 400 recorded "fast days" either by churches or by public authorities in New England between 1620 and 1815.

The "fast-day" became the Church's version of the Solemn Assembly of the Old Testament, calling the Church together to fast and pray in order to confront the urgent problems and crises of that time. Below are just a few examples of these calls to prayer:

• Prior to the founding of our nation, the Continental Congress issued a proclamation recommending "a day of publick [sic] humiliation, fasting, and prayer" be observed on July 20, 1775. [2]

• During the Quasi-War with France, President John Adams declared May 9, 1798 as "a day of solemn humility, fasting, and prayer," during which citizens of all faiths were asked to pray "that our country may be protected from all the dangers which threaten it". [3]

• On March 30, 1863, President Abraham Lincoln issued a proclamation expressing the idea "that the awful calamity of civil war, which now desolates the land, may be but a punishment, inflicted upon us, for our presumptuous sins", and designated April 30, 1863 as a day of "national humiliation, fasting and prayer" in the hope that God would respond by restoring "our now divided and suffering Country to its former happy condition of unity and peace". [4]

He went on to say, "…it is the duty of nations as well as of men, to owe their dependence upon the overruling power of God, to confess their sins and transgressions, in humble sorrow, yet with assured hope that genuine repentance will lead to mercy and pardon; and to recognize the sublime truth, announced in the Holy Scriptures and proven by all history that those nations only are blessed whose God is the Lord." [5]

It is sad to say but true. The practice of fasting within the Church today has greatly diminished through the years and its spiritual significance as an important Christian discipline has almost disappeared. There are many Christians who regard fasting as no longer needed or relevant. Yet, there has never been another time in the history of the Church that it is more needed!

We have God's promise that if He pronounces judgment upon a nation, and that nation turns from their evil; in His mercy, He will not bring the judgment He pronounced upon them. "At what instant I shall speak concerning a nation, and concerning a kingdom, to pluck up, and to pull down, and to destroy it; If that nation, against whom I have pronounced, turn from their evil, I will repent of the evil that I thought to do to them" (Jeremiah 18:7-8).

We have God's promises that when we turn to him in prayer and fasting that He will forgive us and heal our nations, yet, for the most part, the practice of calling Solemn Assemblies or "fast-days" has been forgotten or abandoned in the Church. Only in recent years, with a fresh move of God calling intercessors, churches and nations to set aside specified times to fast and pray, has there been a renewed interest and desire to seek God's face on behalf of cities, people groups and nations.

Just as the children of Israel brought God's judgments upon themselves when they had rebelled and sinned against Him, His judgments will come upon any nation and people who continually turn away from Him, reject His Word and continue in their sins.

I believe that America right now is hanging in the balances! We can choose to continue in the path of rejecting God and turning from the precepts of His Word upon which our nation was founded and experience God's judgments;

America right now is hanging in the balances!

Or, we can hear the call of God's Spirit to "sanctify a fast and call a solemn assembly" humble ourselves before Him in true repentance and experience an unprecedented outpouring of His Spirit.

God's Call to Israel

God put a word in the mouth of the Prophet Joel calling the people to a time of fasting and repentance.

The circumstances were desperate!

Never before had they experienced such devastation on this scale.

They faced dire circumstances far greater than anything they had ever witnessed or had even heard about from their forefathers.

The land was totally desolate!

The palmerworm, locusts, cankerworms and caterpillars had stripped the fields bare. All the vines had dried up and the trees had withered. The seed had rotted under the clods of soil, "The seed is rotten under their clods, the garners are laid desolate, the barns are broken down; for the corn is withered" (Joel 1:17).

Fires had destroyed the pastures and the cattle and sheep were wasting away. The rivers were dried up. Poverty had ravaged the entire country.

Into this scene of total devastation and poverty comes the call from the lips of the prophet, *"Blow the trumpet in Zion, sanctify a fast, call a solemn assembly..."* *(Joel 2:15).* The prophet Joel saw this great devastation as a judgment from God for the sin that had been committed in the nation of Israel. He instructed the priests to blow the trumpets gathering the people together to fast, pray, repent, weep and mourn so they would escape the wrath of God and prepare for the day of judgment.

The Call to Prayer and Fasting was Universal!

When the priests blew the trumpet calling the people together, not a person was to be absent. The old, young children, mothers with infants at their breasts, the bridegroom and bride on their wedding day were all required to assemble before the altar.

The priests, instead of wearing their white priestly robes with brightly colored sashes, were clothed in black goat's hair sackcloth, twisted around them and bound with a rough girdle of the same material, which they never unbound night or day.

> Fasting empowers prayer to push back and repel Satan's darkness, to remove Satan's roadblocks, and to defeat Satan's attacking forces.
> Wesley L. Duewel

Instead of their usual position on the steps and platform on the altar, the priests turned their backs to the altar and lay prostrate on their faces facing the invisible Presence within the sanctuary.

Instead of hymns and music that normally accompanied their prayers, nothing could be heard except the sobs, the passionate cries for mercy, the loud high-pitched "howls" of the people and priests as they repented and mourned for their sins—as the priests beat their breasts and cried out, "Spare thy people, O LORD."

Afterward!

Look with me now at God's promise in Joel 2:28-29 to the children of Israel concerning what would happen as a result of their obedience to humble themselves before Him in fasting and prayer. We have quoted these verses often in reference to an end-time outpouring of God's Spirit upon all flesh. *"And it shall come to pass afterward, that I will pour out my spirit upon all flesh; and your sons and your daughters shall prophesy, your old men shall dream dreams, your young men shall see visions. And also upon the servants and upon the handmaids in those days will I pour out my spirit."*

At Pentecost, when the Holy Spirit descended from Heaven in a rushing mighty wind and cloven tongues of fire upon the 120 gathered in the upper room, it was a fulfillment of this prophecy. Peter had no doubt about what had happened to them that glorious day! He stood to his feet and said, *"...this is that which was spoken by the prophet Joel:..." (Acts 2:16). Ten days they had been gathered together in fasting and prayer, "with one accord in prayer and supplication" (Acts 1:14).*

However, this outpouring of God's Spirit was not a

one-time event! Throughout the years, as God's people have set themselves apart through fasting and prayer seeking an outpouring of His Spirit to empower them in doing God's work, God has heard and answered! In this end time hour before Christ's return, I expect the greatest outpouring of His Spirit far greater than anything the Church has ever experienced. It will come as the Church responds to this end time call to fasting and prayer.

> Prayer and fasting are the keys to the release of the great end-time outpouring of His Spirit.

Notice closely in verse 28 the word *afterward* denoting *when* God's promised outpouring would come. Preceding this promise was a series of at least five admonitions calling the people to prayer and fasting:

1. Joel 1:13

Gird yourselves, and lament, ye priests: howl, ye ministers of the altar; come, lie all night in sackcloth, ye ministers of my God:

2. Joel 1:14

Sanctify ye a fast, call a solemn assembly, gather the elders and all the inhabitants of the land into the house of the LORD your God, and cry unto the LORD.

3. Joel 2:12-13

Therefore also now, saith the LORD, turn ye even to me with all your heart, and with fasting, and with weeping and with mourning: And rend your heart, and not your garments and turn unto the LORD your God;

4. Joel 2: 15-16

Blow the trumpet in Zion, sanctify a fast, call a solemn assembly: Gather the people, sanctify the congregation, assemble the elders, gather the children and those that suck the breasts: let the bridegroom go forth of his chamber, and the bride out of her closet.

5. Joel 2:17-18

Let the priests, the ministers of the LORD, weep between the porch and the altar, and let them say, Spare thy people, O LORD, and give not thine heritage to reproach that the heathen should rule over them: wherefore should they say among the people, Where is their God? Then will the LORD be jealous for his land and pity his people.

All of these admonitions to prayer and fasting lead up to verse 28 and the promise of the outpouring of God's Spirit upon all flesh. The key to the release of a global end time outpouring is found in the word *afterward* in Joel 28.

Something Must Happen First!

First must come repentance, turning, fasting, weeping and interceding before God, *then* will come the release of the outpouring.

The only way we will be able to see our cities and nations transformed; men and women saved, healed and delivered, bondages of drugs, alcohol and sexual perversion broken, is for a great outpouring of God's Spirit to be released upon the Church.

We must strive, contend, fight, and set our faces like a flint to fast and pray until God swings open the windows of heaven and begins to pour out His Spirit upon us. Not in just a trickle or a stream, but like the river of Ezekiel 47 flowing through the Church to bring salvation, healing and deliverance in Jesus' Name!

It is of great importance that you understand that when Joel called Israel together to fast and pray, it was not until AFTER the time of fasting that deliverance was promised. Prayer and fasting were the keys to the release of God's power on their behalf. Joel said, "Then will the LORD be jealous for his land, and pity his people" (Joel 2:18).

Seven Prophetic Promises

God gave seven prophetic promises to the children of Israel of things He would do for them as they responded to this divine call to fasting and prayer. These same seven promises are for God's people today who will give themselves to fasting and prayer.

1. God broke their poverty and divine provision was released! God said, "Behold I will send you corn, and wine, and oil and you shall be satisfied therewith..." (Joel 2:19).

In essence, God was saying He would meet their every need! Are you ready for the chains on your finances to break and to receive God's provision for your every need?

2. As they fasted, God delivered them from the oppression of the enemy! He promised, "But I will remove far off from you the northern army, and will drive him into a land barren and desolate" (Joel 2:29).

As you respond to God's call and begin to set aside seasons of prayer and fasting, believe God's promise to break the stranglehold of the enemy off your family, loved ones and release deliverance to those who are bound.

3. God promised to cause the former and latter rain to come down. He said, "...rejoice in the LORD your God: for he hath given you the former rain moderately, and he will cause to come down for you the rain, the former rain, and the latter rain in the first month" (Joel 2:23).

In this verse God promised to open the widows of heaven and pour out rain into the dry parched land in such abundance that it would be the equivalent of the spring and autumn rains combined! The land would be healed and begin to produce an abundance of crops.

As you sanctify a fast and call a solemn assembly, you don't need to go around with a somber expression or a cast down spirit. God wants you to rejoice because He will open the windows of heaven over your life, your city and nation and begin to pour out the "former and latter rain"…the rain of His power and presence!

> As you set aside times to fast and pray, believe God for these seven prophetic promises.

*4. **God promised that He would prosper His people,** "**And the floors shall be full of wheat, and the fats shall overflow with wine and oil**" (**Joel 2:24**), "**And you shall eat in plenty, and be satisfied…**" (**Joel 2:26**).*

Just as the people of Israel received the overflow—God's superabundance, as they turned to Him through fasting and prayer, He will do the same for you. Not only is God ready to break the chains binding your finances, He desires to bless and prosper you until His blessings and provision are overflowing in your life!

5. God promised to restore what the enemy had stolen! "And I will restore to you the years that the locust hath eaten, the cankerworm, and the caterpillar, and the palmerworm, my great army which I sent among you" (Joel 2:25).

Think about all the things the enemy has stolen from you, your children and family. What about the people in your city and nation that the enemy has held in bondage and is trying to destroy. Jesus said, *"The thief cometh not but for to steal, and to kill, and to destroy:" (John 10:10).* As you set aside times to fast and pray, believe God for restoration in your life. Believe Him to break the bondage of the oppressor off the backs of those bound in shackles of drug and alcohol addiction. Believe Him to set the captives free!

6. God promised that after fasting and prayer would come the outpouring of His Spirit, "And it shall come to pass afterward, that I will pour out my spirit upon all flesh..." (Joel 2:28).

As God's people respond and unite in a global call to prayer and fasting, God will hear from Heaven and we will experience a mighty outpouring of His Spirit! How hungry are you for a fresh outpouring and anointing of God's Spirit upon your life and ministry? Are you ready to pay the price, to humble yourself, repent and cry out to God until you are filled to overflowing with His Spirit?

7. God promised to manifest signs and wonders! He said, "And I will shew wonders in the heavens and in the earth..."(Joel 2:29).

God intends to manifest signs and wonders through His Church! Just as He manifested signs and wonders on behalf of the children of Israel and signs and wonders were a vital part of the early Church, God has planned for signs and wonders to be manifested through believers today in Jesus' Name! Jesus said, *"And these signs shall follow them that believe: In my name shall they cast out devils: they shall speak with new tongues... they shall lay hands on the sick and they shall recover"* *(Mark 16:17-18).*

As the Church unites in seasons of prayer and fasting, God's power and anointing will be released in the powerful dimension Christ intended. Miracles of healing and deliverance will be manifested not just through well-known Christian leaders and ministers, but through an army of men and women in every nation who have received a double-portion anointing of God's Spirit.

Solemn Assemblies were Considered as Holy Unto the Lord

In the Old Testament "Solemn Assemblies" were also referred to as "Holy Convocations". They were times when God's people came together to confess their personal and corporate sins and to seek God in fasting and repentance. In Leviticus 23 and Numbers 28-29 God directs the children of Israel to observe seven days each year as Solemn Assemblies (or Holy Convocations). The Holy Convocation of Leviticus 23:8 is referred to in Deuteronomy 16:8 as a Solemn Assembly. In Leviticus 23:36 the 8th day of the Feast of Tabernacles is called both a Holy Convocation and a Solemn Assembly.

Each of these Solemn Assemblies was related to the seven feasts God established.

1. The first day of the Feast of Passover (the 15th day of the 1st month).

2. The seventh day of the Feast of Passover (the 21st day of the 1st month).

3. The Feast of First Fruits (or Pentecost, coming 50 days after Passover).

4. The Feast of Trumpets (the 1st day of the 7th month).

5. The Day of Atonement (the 10th day of the 7th month).

6. The 1st day of the Feast of Tabernacles (the 15th day of the 7th month).

7. The 8th day of the Feast of Tabernacles (22nd day of the 7th month).

These days were to be considered as holy unto the Lord. The people were not to do any type of work on those days. They were to consecrate those days and keep them as holy convocations, with the major focus of fasting and seeking God.

There are five distinctive characteristics of the Solemn Assemblies:

1. They were mandatory requiring all the children of Israel to participate. This is clearly revealed in Leviticus 23:29 regarding the Solemn Assembly on the Day of Atonement, *"If there is any person who will not humble himself on this same day, he shall be cut off from his people."* This same admonition is found in Exodus 12:15 in connection with the Solemn Assembly for the Feast of Unleavened Bread.

2. The Solemn Assembly and Holy Convocation
was a time of fasting. On the Day of Atonement in
Leviticus 23 the children of Israel were directed to
"afflict their souls" which is a specific reference
to fasting.

3. Solemn Assemblies occurred at regular, specified
times. God planned that the Solemn Assemblies
would coincide with the seven feasts He established
for the children to observe. It was a time when His
people were to gather together to renew their covenant
relationship with Him.

4. The Solemn Assemblies were to be times of
rest when the children of Israel did not work. God
wanted the Solemn Assemblies to be a time when
His people would concentrate their attention upon
their relationship with Him and what He wanted to
accomplish in their lives, instead of being distracted
by their normal activities. The Solemn Assembly
was a time for the people to confess their personal

and corporate sins. Fasting is one of God's major means of causing His people to confront sin in their lives. Sin separates us from God and one another and revival cannot occur without God's people dealing with their sins.

Fasting In Times of Great Adversity

In addition to these Solemn Assemblies associated with God's feasts, there are many more assemblies where the people of God were called together by the leaders, although the specific phrase *Solemn Assembly* is not used. This was the case in 1 Samuel 7:5-6, *"Then Samuel said, 'Gather all Israel to Mizpeh, and I will pray to the Lord for you. And they gathered to Mizpeh, and drew water and poured it out before the Lord, and fasted on that day, and said there, 'We have sinned against the Lord.' And Samuel judged the sons of Israel at Mizpeh.'*

For a moment, consider the desperate circumstances the children of Israel faced. The Philistines had defeated them in battle and had captured the Ark of God. It was eventually returned to them where they placed it in the house of Abinidab in Kirjathjearim where they left it for twenty years. The people of God were so defeated that *"all the house of Israel lamented after the Lord" (1 Samuel 7:2).*

Israel's defeat was the result of years of on-going sin in Israel and in the spiritual leadership. Eli had been the reigning priest and judge. His sons, Hophni and Phinehas were so backslidden—their consciences so seared that they had actually engaged in sexual sin in the Temple! (1 Samuel 2:27-36). God's judgment was pronounced upon both Eli and his sons because of Eli's failure to judge and deal with the sin in his own household. The children of Israel had sinned by following after false gods.

Could it be that we are now experiencing God's judgment upon America because we have turned our backs on God, pushed Him out of our schools, condoned the murder of millions of innocent babies through abortion, condoned homosexuality and a promiscuous lifestyle and have refused to turn back to Him?

Could it be that the Church is not functioning in the powerful spiritual dimension of apostolic power and authority Jesus made possible because there is sin in the camp? Is it because we have failed to deal with the sin that has penetrated the spiritual leadership as well as our failure and negligence in dealing with sin in our churches?

A Call for National Repentance

In this position of defeat and despair, God used Samuel to call the children of Israel to personal and national repentance. He said, *"If ye do return unto the LORD with all your hearts, then put away the strange gods and Ashtaroth from among you, and prepare your hearts unto the LORD, and serve him only: and he will deliver you out of the hand of the Philistines"* *(1 Samuel 7:3).* Israel responded by turning to the Lord and by putting away their false gods.

> Could it be that we are now experiencing God's judgment upon America because we have turned our backs on God?

Notice in this verse that Samuel called the people to turn to the LORD with all their hearts. True repentance is more than just confessing sin or even feeling sorry for sins that have been committed. It requires renouncing sin, turning away from the sin and turning back to God with the whole heart.

Samuel called the people together for a solemn assembly—a season of prayer and fasting. All of Israel gathered together at Mizpeh, a city of Benjamin, "the watch-tower", where the people were accustomed to meet during great national emergencies. It was about four miles north-west of Jerusalem and was situated on a high hill, about 600 feet above the plain of Gibeon.

> God is calling the Church to turn to Him with all our hearts, and with fasting!

This was the beginning of a national revival! As they gathered together three things happened:

1. They drew water and poured it out before the Lord as a drink offering symbolizing their hunger and need for God's Spirit to be poured out upon them.

2. They humbled themselves before God, mourning for their sins.

3. They repented and confessed their personal and national sins. They said, *"We have sinned against the Lord"* (1 Samuel 7:6).

When the Philistines heard that Israel had gathered together at Mizpeh, they decided it was a good time for them to attack. The children of Israel heard the Philistines were coming against them and became fearful. They implored Samuel to intercede before God on their behalf and save them out of the hands of their enemies. Samuel offered up a burnt offering to the Lord and cried out to Him on Israel's behalf. *"And the Lord heard him."* *(1 Samuel 7:9)*

Fasting Brings Heaven's Response!

Praise God! When God's people turn to Him with fasting and prayer, heaven responds! God heard the cry of his fasting, praying people and responded in great power!

Imagine Samuel praying at the altar, with his hands lifted toward the heavens, while the Philistine armies could be seen advancing against Israel. Suddenly, there was a loud thunder from heaven! The Philistines became confused and started running in fear and the Israelites pursued and defeated them, *"but the LORD thundered with a great thunder on that day upon the Philistines, and*

discomfited them; and they were smitten before Israel"
(1 Samuel 7:10).

Notice the results of this season of fasting
and prayer:

1. **Deliverance!** God heard their prayers and
delivered them out of the hands of their enemies. *"So
the Philistines were subdued, and they came no more
into the coast of Israel: and the hand of the LORD
was against the Philistines all the days of Samuel"*
(1 Samuel 7:13).

2. **Restoration**! God restored all the cities that the
Philistines had taken from Israel. (1 Samuel 7:14).

3. **Peace!** *"And there was peace between Israel
and the Amorites" (1 Samuel 7:14).*

God is Calling the Church to Turn to Him with All Our Hearts!

The Spirit of God is saying to the Church: *"...Turn
ye even to me with all your heart, and with fasting, and
with weeping, and with mourning: And rend your heart,*

and not your garments, and turn unto the LORD your God: for he is gracious and merciful, slow to anger, and of great kindness, and repenteth him of the evil" (Joel 2:12-13).

In the Old Testament when the Jews tore their garments, it was a sign of grief and excessive sorrow.

- When Job lost everything including all his sons and daughters, he tore his clothes, shaved his head, fell to the ground and worshipped the Lord. (See Job 1:20-21)

- When the children of Israel sinned against God and were defeated in the battle at Ai, Joshua tore his clothes, fell to the earth, put dust on his head and stayed there until evening. (See Joshua 7:1-6)

It was customary for those who were fasting to tear their garments, clothe themselves in sackcloth and sprinkle ashes on their heads as outward signs of sorrow or mourning. However, it was possible for them to go through the outward motions of fasting without truly being repentant.

The fasting God honors is the fast that begins with the attitude of the heart.

God wants us to *turn* to Him with all our hearts **and with fasting!** Fasting involves humbling ourselves before God, having a genuine sorrow for our sins and having repentant hearts. It also involves a willingness to *turn* from our own ways, from every wrong attitude, every evil thought, every evil desire and everything that is displeasing to Him.

Most of you reading this book know God's promise in 2 Chronicles 7:14 and can quote it from memory. *"If my people, which are called by my name, shall humble themselves, and pray, and seek my face, and turn from their wicked ways; then will I hear from heaven, and will forgive their sin, and will heal their land."*

God's call is to the Church—to His people—to you and me! It must begin with us! We must be willing to rid ourselves of our pride, humble ourselves before God and before one another, as the prophets of old did, and lead the way through seasons of fasting and prayer.

Pastors, evangelists, ministers and Christian leaders must call the people together for a "solemn" assembly. This does not mean there should not be times of praise and rejoicing, but that there should also be specific times set aside by Christian leaders to fast—travail—weep and mourn for the sins of the people.

This is the Call for Repentance Among God's People!

It is my prayer that a spirit of repentance (true repentance that comes from the heart) will sweep through the Church bringing us to our knees! God's people everywhere must unite in praying—crying out to God with one voice, "Spare thy people, O Lord!"

As we prepare for Christ's coming, we need to set ourselves apart in seasons of *personal* fasting and prayer where we are pouring out our hearts, weeping before Him, asking Him to expose all sin in our lives and repenting of our sins.

Then, God wants to bring the Church together in seasons of *corporate* fasting where the Body of Christ unites globally to repent for the sins that have crept into the Church, to seek divine intervention in the desperate conditions in our cities and nations and to believe Him for a great outpouring of His Spirit on a global scale.

Are you desperate for a move of God's Spirit in your life, city and nation?

Are you so hungry for God's presence, power and anointing in your life you are willing to stay on your face before God in fasting and prayer until He pours out His Spirit upon you?

Hear the call of God's Spirit and respond today by making a commitment before God to set yourself apart in seasons of prayer and fasting. Make fasting and prayer part of your lifestyle. Humble yourself before God and repent of all sin. Seek His face with all your heart and believe Him for a mighty move of His Spirit—a global spiritual awakening—a manifestation of His power and glory—and His anointing flowing through you in a double portion of His Spirit.

From the depths of my spirit I urge you to join with me and thousands of Christians worldwide to hear and respond to the call of God's Spirit to "Sanctify a fast… call a solemn assembly".

This is a universal call! If you are really hungry for an outpouring of God's Spirit in your life, city and nation, now is the time to respond!

FASTING
THAT MOVES
GOD'S HAND

Chapter Two

Unleashing the Spiritual 'Atomic Bomb' of Fasting

"Therefore also now, saith the Lord, turn ye even to me
with all your heart, and with fasting and with weeping
and with mourning:"
Joel 2:12

chapter two

Unleashing the Spiritual "Atomic Bomb" of Fasting

God-ordained fasting is one of the greatest spiritual resources available to the Church. Accompanied with fervent prayer and intercession, it is the most dynamic, potent power in the world today!

It is more powerful than any weapon, including nuclear weapons, in the arsenals of the greatest military forces on earth.

It has more power than the power released in the atomic bomb!

Consider some of the following figures related to the atomic bomb. (The Nagasaki and Hiroshima bombs were probably detonated at about 1800 feet altitude.)

"At 2,500 feet from point of impact—if the bomb had reached earth—not from the point of explosion, 1,800 feet above, which would be farther—the pressure exerted was approximately six tons to the square feet.

"At 4,200 feet, the pressure was a little more than one ton per square foot.

"The first pressure noted above, is equivalent to a gale force of wind at 150 miles per hour, multiplied by 133, which equals the pressure of a wind blowing 20,000 miles per hour.

"The second pressure noted is equivalent to 24 times the pressure of a 150-mile gale and equals the pressure of a 3,600-mile-per-hour hurricane.

"These enormous pressures are not wholly instantaneous, but are slightly delayed in their application, giving the water time to partially yield, and hence build up enormous wave effects. A vast, cone-shaped vortex is created, with a terrific "out-thrust", and subsequent return, of the displaced waters. No one can possibly calculate the true extent of this effect, but some physicists have stated that a wave

> Through fasting and prayer, you are able to tap into the unlimited, supernatural power of God!

of great height will be created.

"Consider the effect on water of the temperatures developed. The temperature of the atomic 'Sun' is estimated at four million degrees Fahrenheit.

Combustible materials of all kinds will burn at 1.4 miles distance. The ground temperature below the burst (at 1,800 feet altitude) was certainly more than 1,500 degrees 'Centigrade.' Water was instantly vaporized. Forests were scorched at 8,000 feet distance. All these facts point to the instantaneous vaporization of millions of tons of water, to be thrown far into the upper atmosphere, and thence precipitated in torrential rains in distant parts of the world." [1]

This is the great natural power that man has discovered.

But, even greater still, and even more potent, is the spiritual weapon of prayer and fasting available to every Christian.

We serve the awesome, omnipotent, Jehovah God Almighty Who spoke the worlds into existence. Who said, *"Let there be light: and there was light" (Genesis 1:3).* We serve an unlimited, supernatural God, Who created the sun and moon and flung the stars into space, Who spoke and created the world and every living thing in it; Who formed man from the dust of the earth and breathed into him the breath of life.

The Power of Prayer and Fasting Transends the Laws of Nature!

As we fast and pray, we are able to tap into the unlimited, supernatural power of God!

Moses prayed, struck his staff on the Red Sea and it parted! (Exodus 14:21)

Joshua prayed and the sun and moon stood still! (Joshua 10:12-14)

Elijah prayed and God sent down fire from heaven! (1 Kings 18:31-38)

Elisha prayed and the dead were raised! (2 Kings 4:32-37)

Through fasting:

- Entire nations have been delivered out of the hands of the enemy!

- Nations have turned to God!

- Men have changed the mind of God and averted divine judgment!

- The power and glory of God have been manifested in an outpouring of His Spirit that has swept across nations bringing multiplied thousands into the Kingdom and empowering the Church to work the works of God.

Prayer and Fasting Moves the Hand of God!

Prayer and fasting enables us to move the hand of God! Yet, it is the great unrealized power of the Church and the most neglected and often forgotten spiritual weapon among the great majority of believers. In the past 100 years the Church abandoned the practice of the Solemn Assemblies or fast-days. It hasn't been until recent years that God has begun to stir up the Church with a fresh emphasis on prayer and fasting.

Due to a lack of teaching in our churches, very few

Christians realize the tremendous impact fasting has in the spiritual realm. Others fail to see the need and refuse to discipline their lives to bring the appetites of their bodies into full submission to God for seasons of prayer and fasting.

This is the hour God wants to unleash the 'atomic bomb' of fasting within the Church to enable us to fulfill His will in reaching and winning the lost in our cities and nations.

According to Operation World, the total population of individuals from unreached peoples is 2.84 billion or 41.1% of humanity. [2] That means that almost half of the world's population has never heard the name of Jesus!

We must activate this powerful spiritual force of fasting and prayer to tear down satanic strongholds holding these unreached people groups in bondage and open wide the doors for the Gospel into these unreached areas of the world! Jesus said that before He returns the Gospel must be preached in all the world—which includes the areas now closed to the Gospel. *"And this gospel of the kingdom shall be preached in all the world for a witness unto all nations; and then shall the end come" (Matthew 24:14).*

The only way we will be able to penetrate the spiritual darkness and push back the evil principalities and powers in these unreached areas is through strong, focused prayer and fasting on a global scale! It will take an army of intercessors who know how to wield these powerful spiritual weapons of fasting and prayer.

The Early Church was Empowered Through Fasting

Fasting was a vital part of the early Church. Before the Apostles and leaders made important decisions, faced desperate circumstances or took action on anything that would impact the Church, they fasted and prayed.

In Acts 12 we see how Herod had begun persecuting the Church. After killing James, the brother of John, Herod saw that it pleased the Jews and he arrested Peter with the intention of killing him too. But because it was the Feast of Unleavened Bread (Passover week), Herod postponed Peter's execution and put him in prison, *"and delivered him to four quaternions of soldiers to keep him; intending after Easter (Passover) to bring him forth to the people"* *(Acts 12:4).*

According to the Law, the last day of Passover (the 7th day) was a required Solemn Assembly. The Christians in Jerusalem (most of whom were Jews) were no doubt observing the Solemn Assembly (including fastings and prayers). That evening, following a day of Solemn Assembly, the Church stayed together and we read, *"Peter therefore was kept in prison: but prayer was made without ceasing of the church unto God for him" (Acts 12:5)*

Herod and the sleeping soldiers had no idea that the supernatural, powerful spiritual force of prayer and fasting had been activated. Through prayer and fasting the Church had tapped into a divine power Source. That night as they prayed, God supernaturally intervened.

The Angel of the Lord was dispatched to deliver Peter out of prison. The chains fell off Peter and he walked out of the prison led by the Angel of the Lord while the soldiers slept!

Worship + Prayer + Fasting Activates God's Power

In Acts 13:1-4 we find the church leaders in Antioch uniting in a time of corporate prayer and fasting. We don't know how long they were fasting, but as they prayed and fasted, God spoke to them revealing His will. *"As they ministered to the LORD, and fasted, the Holy Ghost said, Separate me Barnabas and Saul for the work whereunto I have called them. And when they had fasted and prayed, and laid their hands on them, they sent them away"* *(Acts 13:2-3).*

Can you imagine what would happen in the Church today if Christian leaders followed this pattern of prayer and fasting before ordaining pastors, establishing ministers in major leadership positions, appointing worship leaders, selecting teachers, worship teams and other ministry workers? I believe there would be a spiritual revolution! Our churches would be operating in a powerful spiritual dimension of the Holy Spirit greater than anything we have experienced.

There are three powerful spiritual dynamics that were at work: Worship, prayer and fasting. In verse two we read, *"As they ministered to the LORD..."* As they began to worship and pour out their love upon the Lord, and their worship was added to their prayers and fasting, God came down and met with them! He spoke to them through the Holy Spirit giving them specific direction and revealing God's will.

> When worship, prayer and fasting are combined, a powerful flow of God's power is released.

When these three spiritual dynamics: Worship, prayer and fasting are combined together, something begins to happen! God's power and presence are manifested. A powerful flow of God's Spirit is released!

The sick are healed!

Those bound by sin and all types of addictions are set free!

The Church is revived and begins to move in the gifts of the Spirit.

Within the Church in recent years there has been a spiritual revolution taking place with a strong emphasis on worship. On a global scale we are seeing a greater depth and dimension of worship in our churches where believers are breaking through traditional barriers and are being set free to worship the Lord with a new freedom and greater intimacy.

In addition, there has been a massive, global prayer

movement. Multiplied thousands of prayer groups and ministries have been mobilized in almost every country. Twenty-four hour prayer has been activated in prayer towers, small groups and churches around the world. Multiplied millions of Christians are being mobilized to unite in global prayer initiatives.

> Worship + Prayer + Fasting moves the hand of God.

Worship + Prayer + Fasting moves the hand of God and releases His power in our lives! I believe now is the time when God is calling the Church to activate fasting along with this new dimension of worship and prayer. As we do, I believe we will see a mighty spiritual explosion of God's power released in our midst.

Are you ready and willing to move into this powerful dimension by making fasting a vital part of your life?

Fasting that Changed the Course of History!

The prayer and fasting that took place among the leaders in the church at Antioch changed the course of history!

As they prayed and fasted, God spoke clearly to them giving them a directive that would result in a missions movement making Christianity the dominant religion of the Roman Empire within two and a half centuries and would yield 2.2 billion people professing Christianity today with a Christian witness in almost every country. *"As they ministered to the Lord, and fasted, the Holy Ghost said, Separate me Barnabas and Saul for the work whereunto I have called them"* *(Acts 13:2).*

Before this Word from the Holy Spirit, there appears to have been no organized mission of the Church beyond the eastern seacoast of the Mediterranean. Before this Word from the Lord, Paul had not made any missionary journeys westward to Asia Minor, Rome or Spain. He had not written any of his letters, which were all the result of his missionary travels beginning here.

Thirteen out of the 29 books of the New Testament were the result of the ministry that was launched in this moment of prayer and fasting!

Worship, prayer and fasting were the launching pad for a mission that would change the course of world history! The leaders in Antioch received the word of the Lord and obeyed. "And when they had fasted and prayed, and laid their hands on them, they sent them away" (Acts 13:3).

Fasting for Deliverance and Victory!

Throughout the Word we see example after example of how the fasting of God's people moved His hand, brought divine intervention and gave them victory over their enemies. One great example of this is found in 2 Chronicles 20 when the Moabites, Ammonites and the people of Mt. Seir came against Jehoshaphat and the children of Israel.

Notice the very first thing that happened when Jehoshaphat saw the massive armies advancing. He became fearful. *"And Jehoshaphat feared..."(2 Chronicles 20:3)*

The first thing you must face when the enemy is advancing against you—attacking your physical body with sickness and disease, attacking your finances, attacking your marriage, attacking your children—is fear.

When it seems the spiritual forces of darkness in your city or nation are advancing, and in the natural there is no hope—no answers to the desperate circumstances—the first thing you must conquer is a spirit of fear.

Jehoshaphat knew he didn't have the military might or power to meet this challenge and was fearful. But, he didn't give in to his fear or allow it to gain a stronghold. He didn't keep his eyes on his desperate circumstances, but positioned himself for victory by focusing his eyes on Jehovah God Almighty and by calling a fast. Jehoshaphat told God, *"...we have no might against this great company that cometh against us; neither know we what to do: but our eyes are upon you" (2 Chronicles 20:12).*

To position yourself for victory in your desperate circumstances, you must do the same. Jehoshaphat didn't rely on any carnal weapons to defeat his enemies. He didn't summon the top leaders of his army in an effort to develop some sophisticated battle strategies that would help Israel defeat their enemies. He tapped into the supernatural power of God by activating the atomic power of fasting and prayer!

Jehoshaphat Called a Corporate Fast

In verse three we read that Jehoshaphat *"set himself to seek the LORD, and proclaimed a fast throughout all Judah" (2 Chronicles 20:3)*. God's people were called to unite in corporate fasting for divine intervention. Men, women and even the children were included. This call to fast wasn't just to the people in one city. It was to all Judah. The enemies the people of God faced throughout Israel were common enemies. The same threat against one city threatened all of them. When they heard the call to fast, they came from all the cities throughout Judah and gathered together for one purpose: to seek the Lord and ask for His divine intervention. *"And Judah gathered themselves together, to ask help of the LORD: even out of all the cities of Judah they came to seek the LORD" (2 Chronicles 20:4).*

With the people of Judah assembled together for one united purpose, Jehoshaphat led the people in prayer, acknowledging God's mighty power, reminding Him of His covenant with Abraham and His promise of mercy based on His covenant.

As they fasted and prayed, something supernatural

happened! Their fasting and prayer, accompanied by their faith set something in motion in the spirit realm! God spoke to the people through Jahaziel, one of the Levites. The Spirit of God came upon him and used him to give a powerful prophetic word of encouragement and divine direction.

In the circumstances and seemingly impossible situations you face, when you fast and pray, expect God to speak to you. Expect to receive His direction. Then, when you act in faith upon the word of the Lord, you are positioning yourself to win the victory.

> When you fast and pray, expect to receive God's direction.

God's message to Jehoshaphat and the children of Israel was, *"Be not afraid nor dismayed by reason of this great multitude, for the battle is not your's, but God's"* *(2 Chronicles 20:15).* In the great battles and challenges we face against the enemy in our schools, governments, cities and nations, God wants it to be clearly understood that the battles are not our's. They are His battles. Just as He entered into a Covenant with Moses and the children of Israel and promised, *"I will be an enemy unto thine enemies, and an adversary unto thine adversaries" (Exodus 23:22);* He will be an enemy unto our enemies and will fight for us!

When we receive a full revelation that He is with us and is fighting for us, we will not be fearful, but we will stand against the enemy, like Jehoshaphat and the children of Israel, knowing God will give us total victory!

God Gave Jehosaphat a Three-Point Battle Strategy for Victory

God exposed the enemies location and then told Jehoshaphat and the people assembled together they weren't going to have to fight the battle. In verse 17 we see the three point battle strategy God gave them, *'Ye shall not need to fight in this battle: set yourselves, stand ye still, and see the salvation of the LORD with you, O Judah and Jerusalem: fear not, nor be dismayed; tomorrow go out against them: for the LORD will be with you" (2 Chronicles 17:17)*

Their three-point battle strategy was:

81

1. To position themselves and face their enemies knowing the battle was God's and that He would fight for them.

2. To not be fearful or dismayed.

3. To go out against their enemies knowing God was with them.

Upon hearing this word from the Lord, Jehoshaphat and the people received the message and responded with spontaneous worship. They fell on their faces and worshipped God. The Levites and the appointed singers stood up and began to praise *the Lord God of Israel with a loud voice on high*(*2 Chronicles 20:19).* Jehoshaphat appointed singers and sent them out before the army praising God and as they went, God defeated their enemies for them.

Remember: Worship + Prayer + Fasting moves the hand of God and releases His power in our lives!

It wasn't necessary for the children of Israel to use any military weapons. God brought confusion on their enemies and they turned against one another. Their enemies were totally defeated and not one survived! God not only fought for them, He gave them the spoils of war. They had such superabundance it took three days for them to gather all the spoils and they returned to Jerusalem *"with joy; for the LORD had made them to rejoice over their enemies" (2 Chronicles 20:27).*

This tremendous, supernatural victory was won because Jehoshaphat and the children of Israel did not rely on carnal, fleshly weapons but upon powerful spiritual weapons: corporate fasting, united prayer and worship! Paul said, *"For the weapons of our warfare are not carnal, but mighty through God to the pulling down of strongholds" (2 Corinthians 12:4).*

These same spiritual weapons activated by Christians today will bring victories as powerful as they gained for Jehoshaphat and the children of Israel.

We know that our warfare is not a natural warfare. Paul said, *"For we wrestle not against flesh and blood, but against principalities, against powers, against the rulers of the darkness of this world, against spiritual wickedness in high places" (Ephesians 6:12).* In our cities and nations we are waging a spiritual warfare against the rulers and principalities of darkness in this world that are even more formidable than the massive armies that came against Jehoshaphat and the people of God.

Satan, knowing his time is short, has unleashed his fury against the Church of Jesus Christ and every committed Christian yielded to the Lordship of Jesus Christ. His objective is to kill, steal and destroy! Anti-christ spirits and forces are at work today in an attempt to weaken and dilute the message of the Gospel, discredit the work of God, stop the progress of the Church and remove all possible Christian influence from every area of our society.

> This is not a time for the Church to be divided by denominational and doctrinal issues.

This is not a time for the Church to be divided by denominational and doctrinal issues. It is time for all of God's people worldwide to unite in seasons of fasting and prayer believing God for His supernatural divine intervention and an outpouring of His Spirit that will empower us to defeat the enemy and take the victories that belong to us in our personal lives, in our communities, cities and nations.

Prayer and Fasting Changed History at the Battle of Dunkirk

In May of 1940, the prime minister of Britain, Neville Chamberlain resigned and Winston Churchill became his replacement. Adolph Hitler and his army had already invaded and conquered Poland, Norway, Denmark, Holland, Luxembourg and Belgium. The French Army, along with large numbers of English soldiers tried to stop the oncoming army, but after 40 days of fighting, the Allied forces were completely routed. They retreated as far as the English Channel.

More than 330,000 British and French troops became trapped in a tiny coastal enclave known as Dunkirk, with the German Army advancing, only 15 miles away and German airplanes bombing Dunkirk. A defeat there would have likely meant the fall of France, Britain and ultimately all of Europe.

The situation seemed hopeless as the men sent out desperate calls for help. It looked as if they were either going to be imprisoned or killed in a matter of days. Even the military leaders thought very little could be done to rescue more than a few thousand men.

In that seemingly impossible situation, the call to prayer was heard. On May 23, 1940 the call went forth from the churches in Britain and King George VI for a National Day of Prayer to be held on Sunday, May 26. During this time, Rees Howells, one of the most powerful intercessors of our day, also was leading a group of intercessors to pray for England and the allied troops. In his journal entry the day prior to the call to prayer, Reese said, "The world is in a panic today and certainly we would be too unless we were sure the Lord has spoken to us. The destiny of England will be at stake today and tomorrow. In a battle such as we are in today, you cannot trust in a meeting or in feelings. We must go back to what God has told us. There is an enemy that we must keep in check until God does the big thing."

May 24, one day after the call for a National day of prayer, Hitler ignored the advice of many of his generals and ordered his armies to hold their positions while Dunkirk was bombed and shelled from the air and from a distance. Thunderstorms and thick fog made it difficult for the planes to fly or see.

On the National Day of Prayer on May 26, churches

were filled as people from all walks of life sought God for divine intervention to protect and save their friends, loved ones and country. Prime Minister Winston Churchill attended a packed prayer service at Westminster Abbey.

That evening, a daring rescue mission codenamed Operation Dynamo began. Every available vessel down to the smallest fishing boat answered the call to cross the English Channel and rescue the soldiers. It should have taken 40 days. But, in only nine days, 338,000 Allied forces were evacuated. Something had prevented the Germans from overwhelming them on the beaches, and a looming storm from hitting the area. Everyone, including the press, called it a miracle of God.

> Prayer and fasting brought Great Britain from imminent destruction and defeat to a position of great victory.

The prayer and fasting of the people moved the hand of God to intervene at this turning point in Britain's history. It brought them from imminent destruction and defeat to a position of great victory.

With all my heart I believe God will do it again! America has reached perhaps what could be considered its most challenging and dangerous periods in our history. We face the threat of terrorists from within and without, an economic crisis in which we are on a downward spiral, the threat of a nuclear war, and a great spiritual dearth where Christian values upon which this nation was founded have been thrown out. A spiritual war is raging for the soul of this country and if we will hear God's call to prayer and fasting, He will hear and will turn this nation around!

The Power of Prayer and Fasting that Shaped History During the War in North Africa 1941 to 1943

In his book, *Shaping History Through Prayer and Fasting*, dynamic Christian teacher and leader Derek Prince, who has graduated and gone on to receive his heavenly reward, shares the following experience of the power of prayer and fasting to shape history during the war in North Africa from 1941 to 1943.

I served as a hospital attendant with the British forces in North Africa. I was part of a small medical unit that worked with two British armored divisions—the

First Armored Division and the Seventh Armored Division.

At that time, the morale of the British forces in the desert was very low. The basic problem was that the men did not have confidence in their officers. As a group, the officers in the desert at that time were selfish, irresponsible, and undisciplined. Their main concern was not the well-being of the men, or even the effective prosecution of the war, but their own physical comfort.

At that period, our greatest hardship was the shortage of water. Supplies were very strictly rationed. Our military water bottles were filled every other day. This was all the water that we were allowed for every purpose—washing, shaving, drinking, cooking, etc. Yet the officers in their mess each evening regularly consumed more water with their whiskey than was allotted to the other ranks for all purposes combined.

> Prayer and fasting shaped history during the war in North Africa from 1941-1943

The result of all this was the longest retreat in the history of the British army—about seven hundred miles in all—from a place in Tripoli called El Agheila to El Alamein, about fifty miles west of Cairo.

About eighteen months previously, in a military barrack room in Britain, I had received a very dramatic and powerful revelation of Christ. I thus knew in my own experience the reality of God's power. I early came to see that, by New Testament standards, fasting was a normal part of Christian discipline. During the whole period that I was in the desert, I regularly set aside Wednesday of each week as a special day for fasting and prayer.

During the long and demoralizing retreat to the gates of Cairo, God laid on my heart a burden for prayer, both for the British forces in the desert and for the whole situation in the Middle East. Yet, I could not see how God could bless leadership that was so unworthy and inefficient. I searched in my heart for some form of prayer that I could pray with genuine faith and that would cover the needs of the situation. After a while, it seemed that the Holy Spirit gave me this prayer: "Lord, give us leaders such that it will be for Your glory to give us victory through them."

I continued praying this prayer every day. In due

course, the British government decided to relieve the commander of their forces in the desert and to replace him with another man. The man whom they chose was a general named W. H. E. "Strafer" Gott. He was flown to Cairo to take over command, but he was killed when his plane was shot down. At this critical juncture, the British forces in this major theater of the war were left without a commander. Winston Churchill, then Prime Minister of Britain, proceeded to act largely on his own initiative.

He appointed a more-or-less unknown officer, named B. L. Montgomery, who was hastily flown out from Britain.

He was just and God-fearing. He was also a man of tremendous discipline. Within two months, he had instilled a totally new sense of discipline into his officers and had thus restored the confidence of the men in their leaders.

Then the main battle of El Alamein was fought. It was the first major allied victory in the entire war up to that time. The threat to Egypt, the Suez Canal, and Palestine was finally thrown back, and the course of the war changed in favor of the Allies. Without a doubt, the battle of El Alamein was the turning point of the war in North Africa.

Two or three days after the battle, I found myself in the desert a few miles behind the advancing Allied forces. A small portable radio beside me on the tail-board of a military truck was relaying a news commentator's description of the scene at Montgomery's headquarters as he had witnessed it on the eve of the battle. He recalled how Montgomery publicly called his officers and men to prayer, saying, "Let us ask the Lord, mighty in battle, to give us the victory."

As these words came through that portable radio, God spoke very clearly to my spirit, "That is the answer to your prayer." I believe that the prayer that God gave me at that time could well be applied to other situations, both military and political: "Lord, give us leaders such that it will be for Your glory to give us victory through them."[1]

Fasting Supercharges Our Prayers and Activiates God's Power

God's Word reveals an undeniable record of the awesome power of God being released as His people fast

92

and pray. Through the power of God-ordained fasting:

- We are able to pull down satan's strongholds in our cities and nations.

- We can walk in the powerful realm Jesus taught where nothing is impossible!

- We can win great personal victories over our enemies.

- We can experience healing and restoration.

- We can walk in revelation knowledge.

- We can intervene and change the mind of God on behalf of cities and nations.

Knowing that fasting supercharges our prayers and activates God's power on our behalf, my question is; "Why hasn't the Church fully activated this powerful force to take the victories we desperately need in our personal lives, cities and nations?

My friend, have you experienced first-hand the awesome atomic power of fasting in your own personal life?

Jesus Revealed the Importance and Power of Prayer and Fasting

The Word of God contains tremendous examples of individual and corporate fasts and the breakthroughs that resulted. However, the greatest example and teaching we have concerning fasting is found in the life of Jesus. Not only did Jesus go on a 40-day fast before beginning His ministry and before He performed any miracles, He taught about the importance and power of fasting.

In Matthew, chapter seventeen, we read about Peter, James and John and their supernatural experience on the mountain where Christ was transfigured before them. They saw the awesome manifestation of God's glory shining on His face as the sun, His clothes glistening white, radiating a glorious heavenly light. They saw Moses and Elijah talking with Jesus and were overshadowed by a cloud of God's glory. And they

> Have you experienced first-hand the awesome atomic power of fasting in your own personal life?

94

heard the audible voice of God declaring, *"This is my beloved Son, in whom I am well pleased; hear ye him"* (Matthew 17:5).

I am sure that as they left the mountain top and walked with Jesus on the rocky terrain down the mountainside, they were still filled with awe and were meditating on the glorious vision and revelation they had just seen. In chapter four we will take a more in depth look at Jesus' example and teaching on fasting. However, I want to focus a moment on a major incident—a power crisis—the disciples faced where Jesus clearly revealed that the key to walking in God's power is prayer and fasting.

Immediately upon their descent from the mountain and this glorious experience, they came upon a multitude and were confronted by the inability of the disciples to cast a demon out of a young boy. Jesus was met by the father of the boy who fell at Jesus feet crying out for mercy and desiring Him to heal his boy. He told Jesus, *"I brought him to thy disciples, and they could not cure him"* (Matthew 17:16).

The Disciples Faced a Power Crisis

For a moment, let us consider this power crisis and their inability to cast the demon out of the boy. At that point, Jesus had already given His disciples His authority and power. In Matthew, Chapter 10 we read, *"And when he had called unto him his twelve disciples, he gave them power against unclean spirits, to cast them out, and to heal all manner of sickness and all manner of disease"* (Matthew 10:1). He had commissioned them, *"...as ye go, preach, saying, The kingdom of heaven is at hand: Heal the sick, cleanse the lepers, raise the dead, cast out devils: freely ye have received, freely give"* (Matthew 10:7-8).

Jesus also had sent out an additional seventy disciples ahead of Him into the cities where He planned to go. They also received delegated authority to heal the sick and cast out devils. When the seventy returned to Jesus they were overjoyed and reported, *"...even the devils are subject to us through your name"* (Luke 10:17). He then reinforced the fact that He had given them, *"power over all the power of the enemy..."* (Luke 10:19).

The disciples had been going throughout the country healing the sick and casting out devils in His Name. Yet, when they prayed for this boy they had been unable to cast the demon out.

Why weren't they able to cast the demon out?

What was the root cause of the problem for their lack of power?

"This Kind Goeth Not Out but by Fasting and Prayer"

After rebuking them for their unbelief, Jesus directed them to bring the boy to Him. He rebuked the devil, cast it out and the boy was totally healed. Later, the disciples, who were no doubt surprised and perplexed at their lack of power, came privately to Jesus and asked Him why they couldn't cast the demon out.

Notice that Jesus didn't sugarcoat the truth, but told them plainly it was because of their unbelief! Then He said, *"If ye have faith as a grain of a mustard seed, ye shall say unto this mountain, Remove hence to yonder place; and it shall remove; and nothing shall be impossible to you"* *(Matthew 17:20).*

We often quote this familiar verse to emphasize a dimension of faith where Jesus said nothing would be impossible to us! However, Jesus did not stop at verse 20, He continued by saying, "Howbeit this kind goeth not out but by prayer and fasting" (Matthew 17:21). In this verse Jesus reveals the key to walking in the awesome faith and power of Almighty God—prayer and fasting!

> Jesus revealed the key to walking in faith and in the awesome power of Almighty God—prayer and fasting!

We are Facing a Power Crisis in the Church Today!

The time has come when we must take an honest look at the true condition of the Church today!

Can we truthfully say that the power of Almighty God is flowing through the Church in the same dimension as it did in the early Church? Or, are we spiritually impotent, like the disciples who weren't able to cast the demon out of this boy?

Pastors, Christian leaders and ministers within the fivefold ministry, we must not be afraid to face the current power crisis in the Church head-on! It's time for us to humble ourselves before God, repent and ask God to forgive our unbelief.

It is time to get real!

We have built large mega churches with well-organized outreaches and ministries reaching into our cities and nations. But, if the Church is operating in the same powerful dimension Jesus said, where nothing is impossible to us, why are there so many sick people filling our pews?

Why are there so many demon-possessed people walking the streets?

With all the advanced technologies available today, why haven't we taken our cities and nations for God?

Is the power of God being manifested through your life in the dimension Jesus said would be possible for all those who believe?

Allow Jesus' words to resound through the heavens and go deep into your spirit. He said, *"And these signs shall follow them that believe: In my name shall they cast out devils; they shall speak with new tongues...they shall lay hands on the sick and they shall recover."* *"...He that believeth on me, the works that I do shall he do also; and greater works than these shall he do; because I go unto my Father. And whatsoever ye shall ask in my name, that will I do, that the Father may be glorified in the Son"* *(John 14:12-13).*

Jesus made it clear that this power comes through prayer and fasting, *"...this kind does not go out except by prayer and fasting".*

When we reclaim our inheritance as the sons and daughters of God and begin to seek His face in prayer and fasting, all the miracles of the Gospels and the book of Acts will come back into the every day existence in the Church!

Regardless of who you are, if you are born again by the Spirit of God, you are one of His children and through the same power and anointing of the Holy Spirit you are able to do the same works Jesus did! Christ intends for you to also heal the sick and cast out devils in His Name!

Well-known Christian leader, Andrew Murray, said concerning prayer and fasting, "Prayer is reaching out after the unseen; fasting is letting go of all that is seen and temporal. Fasting helps express, deepen, confirm the resolution that we are ready to sacrifice anything, even ourselves to attain what we seek for the kingdom of God." [3]

There are times when the Lord desires to draw us aside; as He did with Peter, James and John on the mountain, so that He can reveal Himself more fully to us. He longs for us to shut out every distraction and shut ourselves in with Him so that He can speak to us. As we wait upon Him, humbling ourselves in His Presence through prayer and fasting, we are changed into His image. *"But we all, with open face beholding as in a glass the glory of the Lord, are changed into the same image from glory to glory, even as by the Spirit of the Lord"* (2 Corinthians 3:18).

> Is the power of God being manifested through your life in the dimension Jesus said would be possible?

Is there a growing hunger in your heart to know

Christ in all His fullness—to be conformed into His image—to be drawn into a closer relationship with Him? It is through seasons of prayer and fasting—waiting in the Lord's presence—that we let go of earthly things and take hold of the eternal.

You can remain where you are, spiritually impotent and unable to do the works Jesus said you would do. Or, you can walk and live in that dimension of power Christ has made possible as you activate the power of fasting in your life.

The decision is yours.

How hungry are you for God?

FASTING
THAT MOVES
GOD'S HAND

Chapter Three

What is True Biblical Fasting?

"If my people, who are called by my name, will humble themselves and pray and seek my face and turn from their wicked ways, then will I hear from heaven and will forgive their sin and will heal their land."
2 Chronicles 7:14

chapter three

What is True Biblical Fasting?

Through the years the Church has experienced powerful manifestations of God's Presence where His glory came down. But, what we are going to see before Christ's return will be on an even greater scale than any previous manifestation of His glory and will be revealed in every nation.

The major keys to the release of this awesome move of God are prayer and fasting. As I have shared in previous chapters, there has been a recent dynamic move of the Spirit with literally thousands of prayer initiatives and prayer networks being established worldwide. However, we cannot and must not stop here. We need to unleash the power of prayer through a renewed emphasis on Biblical fasting.

My Forty-Day Fast

I have personally experienced tremendous breakthroughs in my life and ministry as I have set aside time to fast and seek God's face. As long as I live, I will never forget the night God's shekinah glory came down in one of my meetings in Knoxville, Tennessee. Thinking back upon that night it is impossible for me to adequately describe the tremendous power and glory of God we experienced. It was one of the most awesome events of my life!

> We are creatures of the senses; fasting helps to express, to deepen, and to confirm the resolution that we are ready to sacrifice anything, to sacrifice ourselves, to attain what we seek for the kingdom of God.
> – Andrew Murray

I had just completed a forty-day fast. I ate nothing and drank only water during the entire forty days of my fast.

During the fast, I moved into a new dimension of God's power and anointing and incredible miracles happened in my life. The Holy Spirit directed a number of people to me who were demon-possessed and they received their deliverance. Some were delivered even as

I prayed for them by telephone! Individuals from various states called asking for deliverance and each one of them was set free.

The night of our Crusade in Knoxville was the fortieth day of my fast. The meeting was in a city auditorium where all the Full Gospel churches had come together. The large facility was packed with people eager to receive their miracle.

I had lost a great deal of weight and was just skin and bones. Because of my weakened condition, I remained backstage until it was time for me to preach. The pastor who introduced me warned the people, "Do not be shocked when Brother Lowery comes to minister. He is not sick; he has just concluded a forty-day fast."

When it was time for me to minister, the Chairman of the Crusade helped me to the platform and gave me a tall chair upon which I could lean while I preached. When I walked to the pulpit, I heard a collective gasp as the people observed how emaciated I appeared to them.

I began speaking, softly, since I was extremely weak. As I talked, the Spirit of God gripped the audience as I have never witnessed in my ministry.

I had only been speaking for about ten minutes when suddenly the spiritual atmosphere changed and became so heavy until it was difficult to breathe. Like the charge of an electrical current, the room was charged with the Presence of God. The Holy Spirit began to wash over the congregation like an incoming tide.

Hundreds were Saved and Filled with the Holy Spirit!

A cloud of God's shekinah glory literally came down into that auditorium! Several people saw this glory cloud. When I saw the glory of God come down, I knew without any doubt we were standing on holy ground!

What an awesome sight!

I could see the cloud of God's glory suspended over the heads of the people.

I watched as it moved from one side of the building to the other.

Everywhere the cloud moved, people fell under the power of God, without anyone touching them! All over the auditorium, people were falling under the power of God. People's lives were radically changed and many were healed! It was one of the most glorious sights and experiences I have ever had.

When I had ministered for a short while, I invited those who needed to be saved to stand to their feet and hundreds of men, women and young people leaped up to receive Christ as Savior.

We prayed the sinner's prayer together and there was an immediate outburst of praise from those who had committed their lives to Christ.

I then asked those who wanted to be filled with the Spirit to stand and raise their hands.

Again, there was a tremendous response.

I asked them to repeat a prayer inviting the Spirit into their lives and instructed them, "When I say, 'Be filled with the Holy Ghost!' expect Him to come in."

It happened!

Hundreds were filled with the Spirit and began to speak in tongues as the Spirit gave utterance.

God's Miracle Power Swept Through the Auditorium!

At that moment, I felt led to minister to the sick.

I simply asked those who needed a miracle to stand; if they were in wheelchairs or on cots, they were to place their left hand where the pain or affliction was and lift their right hand.

The service was marked by such intensity and faith that I knew God would move in a remarkable way.

I prayed in a low voice, asking for God's healing presence.

Suddenly, God's power swept over the audience like a wind! It was glorious!

Hundreds were healed. People leaped from wheelchairs and got off cots and began dancing and rejoicing!

Blind eyes were opened.

Deaf ears were unstopped.

Heart conditions, diabetes and other conditions were immediately healed through the marvelous manifestation of God's presence.

Many times throughout my ministry I have experienced a tremendous release of God's power with all types of miracles being manifested as I have given myself to fasting and prayer. I have received revelation knowledge, personal breakthroughs in my life and ministry, financial breakthroughs and God's direction and wisdom in major challenges I have faced as I have humbled myself before God in fasting and prayer. God is not a respecter of persons. He will do the same for you.

What is True Biblical Fasting?

To unleash the power of fasting in your life, in your ministry and your circumstances, you must first understand what true Biblical fasting is, its purpose and how to fast according to the guidelines God has established in His Word.

I do not want to just produce another book on fasting containing more man-made ideas and concepts concerning this vitally important spiritual weapon.

It is my desire that as you read, the Spirit of Almighty God will release fresh revelation knowledge that will forever change your life.

Let us begin our spiritual journey by gaining an understanding of what true Biblical fasting involves. In the Church today there are those who consider abstaining from certain foods, giving up television or other forms of entertainment, or practicing self-denial in other areas of their lives as a type of fast. However, the Word is clear:

> We must never become legalistic in the matter of fasting.

Biblical fasting is abstaining from eating food for a specific period of time for a spiritual purpose.

In the Church today there are many who consider eating only certain foods or juices as being a form of fasting. They use Daniel's three weeks of fasting in Daniel, chapter ten as a reference and eat vegetables only. Daniel said, *"In those days I Daniel was mourning three full weeks. I ate no pleasant bread; neither came flesh nor wine in my mouth, neither did I anoint myself at all, till three whole weeks were fulfilled"* (Daniel 10:1-3).

I have no problem with those who choose to go on a "Daniel fast" eating only vegetables and fruits. However, I personally believe that we need to take a closer look at these verses and take them into context. Three weeks Daniel was mourning and confessing the sins of the people. He was clothed in sackcloth and ashes, which was an outward sign of fasting. In verse three when he said he didn't eat any "pleasant bread", didn't eat meat and drank no wine, and didn't anoint himself, I believe he was merely emphasizing the fact that during this time, he was fasting—abstaining from eating—as he humbled himself in repentance on behalf of the sins of the people. There is no indication in this verse that he ate anything during that time.

Biblical Fasting Means No Food!

The noun translated fast or fasting is *tsom* in the Hebrew and *nesteia* in the Greek language. These words refer to the voluntary abstinence from food. The literal Hebrew translation would be "not to eat." The literal Greek means "no food." I believe true Biblical fasting is abstaining from food, drinking water only. There are also rare occasions when a person goes on an "Absolute" or "Complete" fast where he does not eat or drink water. This was the type of fast Queen Esther and the Jews in Shushan observed as they faced destruction. (See Esther 4:15-17).

We must never become legalistic in the matter of fasting. The most important thing is to be led by His Spirit when you fast. Refuse to allow your natural physical limitations to hinder you from making fasting part of your lifestyle. As you take a step of faith by setting aside one or two days each week to fast, you will experience God's power and presence in a greater way than ever before. You will have a new sensitivity to the Spirit and experience a deeper level of communion with the Lord.

In his spiritual classic, *With Christ in the School of Prayer*, Andrew Murray states, "Faith needs prayer for its full growth. And prayer needs fasting for its full growth; this is the second lesson. Prayer is the one hand with which we grasp the invisible; fasting, the other, with which we let loose and cast away the visible."[1]

In Biblical fasting, our major goal must be to seek God. As we abstain from food we are denying our flesh and bringing it into submission to the Spirit. Our spiritual focus changes where we are letting go of worldly desires and setting our focus on God and the things of the Spirit. It is a time of drawing near to God with all our hearts, souls and bodies.

True Biblical Fasting is Much More Than Just a Religious Exercise

Fasting as a religious exercise has been practiced since ancient times and is found in almost all religions. As early as 950 B.C. the Greeks practiced religious fasting to ward off evil spirits and to mourn the death of friends or relatives. The Greeks believed that upon the death of an individual, demons could enter the living by means of food and drink. So they fasted and mourned.

Fasting in the Old Testament

Throughout the Old Testament there are numerous examples of individual and corporate fasts. As we look closely at some of these fasts in upcoming chapters, you will understand the various reasons why the Old Testament Saints fasted and the reasons why Christians should fast today.

In addition to the fast on the Day of Atonement prescribed by Mosaic Law (See Leviticus 16:29-31; 23:26-32), there were four additional fast days established after the Captivity commemorating the four main events related to the destruction of the first Temple. However, these times of fasting were not prescribed by the Law: The fast of the fourth month (Tammuz), of the fifth month (Ab), of the seventh month (Tishri), and of the tenth month (Tebet). (See Zechariah 8:19)

Two additional fasts were added and are commonly observed by Jews today:

• The Fast of Esther, Adar 13, commemorates the three days that Esther fasted before approaching King Ahasuerus on behalf of the Jewish people. This fast is connected with Purim.

• The Fast of the Firstborn, Nissan 14, is a fast observed only by firstborn males, commemorating the fact that firstborn males were saved from the plague of the firstborn in Egypt. (See Exodus 11:4-7) It is observed on the day preceding Passover.

Among the fasts recorded in the Old Testament we discover that the Old Testament Saints fasted on many different occasions for different purposes:

• Moses fasted 40 days twice: The first 40-day fast, he communed with God and received divine revelation and the 10 commandments. (Deuteronomy 9:9-11) The second 40-day fast he interceded on behalf of the children of Israel so that God wouldn't destroy them. (Exodus 24:18, 25).

• Ezra fasted for God's protection (Ezra 8:21-23), and in mourning because of the people who had been taken captive (Ezra 10:6).

• Elijah fasted 40 days on his way to Mt. Horeb. (1 Kings 19:8).

• Daniel fasted for the fulfillment of God's promises and in repentance for the sins of the people (Daniel 9:3, 20).

• The king and people of Ninevah fasted in repentance to escape God's judgment. (Jonah 3:5-10).

• Solomon humbled himself in fasting and prayer and God greatly increased his wealth and gave him wisdom. (1 Kings 3:10-13).

• Esther fasted on behalf of the Jews so that they would not be destroyed. (Esther 4:15-16).

Fasting Durning the Inter-Testamental Period

As the Old Testament closed, approximately 400 years before the coming of Christ, genuine faith in Israel had been replaced by legalism. During this inter-testamental period, Judaism had elevated ritual fasting to such prominence until secular historians regarded fasting as one of the marks of a genuine Jew. Judaism regarded ritual fasting as a virtuous act that earned the favor of God, regardless of one's heart. As we will see in an upcoming chapter, it was this attitude of legalism that Jesus condemned among the Pharisees as He taught on fasting.

Fasting in the New Testament Church

Fasting was a regular practice in the New Testament Church. During the first four centuries of the Church there were no set rules or regulations concerning fasting. The early Christians practiced various forms of fasting, some of which they took from Jewish customs and others they developed themselves.

- Anna, the Prophetess fasted. She "served God with fastings and prayers night and day" (Luke 2:37).

- Jesus began His ministry with a forty-day fast. (Luke 4:1-2).

- John the Baptist and his disciples fasted. (Matthew 9:14).

- Paul fasted. (Acts 9:9, 11), (Acts 14:19-23) (2 Corinthians 11:27).

- The Prophets and teachers in Antioch fasted. (Acts 13:2-4)

- Cornelius fasted. (Acts 10:30)

By the beginning of the second century A.D. many Christians fasted twice each week on Wednesday and Fridays in order to distinguish themselves from the Jews who fasted on Mondays and Thursdays. Epiphanus, Bishop of Salamis, wrote in the fourth century and said: "Who does not know that Christians all over the world fast and pray on the fourth and sixth day?" In the fourth century it had become customary for those desiring to be baptized to fast on Friday and Saturday before their baptism on Easter Sunday.

History records that believers fasted on Wednesday to remember the day of Jesus' arrest and on Friday to commemorate the day of His crucifixion. By the late fourth century the Church had established the "fast of forty" referring to the forty days of Lent leading up to Easter. At the time of the Reformation (in the late 1400's) the Church, which by that time was represented by the Catholic Church, took the traditions and principles of fasting that had been established by the Church in its first four centuries and turned them into ritualistic and legalistic observances.

Fasting Practices Among Major Religions

Fasting as a mere act of abstaining from food in self denial or as a form of spiritual discipline does not produce spiritual breakthrough. Neither does strict adherence to legalistic doctrines nor the religious practices concerning fasting found in many major religions move God's hand.

In the Catholic Church, fasting is regarded as a form of penance (a pathway for the sinner to seek forgiveness) and an opportunity to grow closer to God. Catholicism requires Eucharistic fasting, which calls for those desiring to take communion to fast food

> By the late 1400's the practice of fasting in the Church had been turned into ritualistic and legalistic observances.

and drink (except water) three hours before they receive communion. Fasting is observed throughout the 40 days of Lent, Ash Wednesday and Good Friday. Every Friday is also designated as a day of abstinence—eating no meat—only fish.

In the Islamic faith, fasting in the month of Ramadan is one of the pillars of their faith. One full month every year fasting is prescribed for Muslims all over the world. Fasting begins at dawn and ends at sunset. During this period one is expected to abstain from all food and drink.

In the Baha'i faith, there is a 19-day period each year when Baha'is fast from sunrise to sunset each day from

March 2-20. This fast also involves complete abstention from food and drink from sunrise until sunset.

Hindus fast on certain days of the month. Days of the week are marked for fasting depending upon the person's favorite god or goddess. For example, on Saturday people fast to appease the god of that day, Shani or Saturn while some fast on Tuesday for the monkey god.

This type of ritualistic fasting is nothing more than a futile exercise and an attempt to obtain righteousness through works. True Biblical fasting involves humbling oneself and seeking after Jehovah, the only true and living God.

There are also people who practice fasting solely for weight loss and who use juice fasts as a natural method of detoxification. While there are proven health benefits from fasting, this is not the objective of true Biblical fasting.

True Biblical Fasting is More Than Self-Denial

True Biblical fasting is not a form, a ritual nor a

mere act of self-denial. It is more than an act of the natural man—more than a matter of not eating for a specified time. It is a spiritual act—originating in our spirits. It involves humbling ourselves before God, genuine sorrow for our sins and a repentant heart. Therefore, our emphasis in fasting must not be upon the outward work of the natural man, but the inward work of God's Spirit in us.

True Biblical fasting is not a manipulative tool to get something from God. Fasting does not change God. It changes us! It is not twisting God's arm to get him to do our bidding but positions ourselves to receive from Him.

We don't fast to earn something from God, but we fast to make connection with Him. In his book, *Fasting*, Jentezen Franklin gives the following definition of Biblical fasting. "Stated simply, biblical fasting is refraining from food for a spiritual purpose. Fasting has always been a normal part of a relationship with God. As expressed by the impassioned plea of David in Psalm 42, fasting brings one into a deeper, more intimate and powerful relationship with the Lord."[2]

> Fasting does not change God. It changes us!

While it is true that our prayers are supercharged through our fasting and that God responds in meeting our needs, true Biblical fasting is not just a spiritual discipline for bringing problems to God to be fixed. It must be, first and foremost, an expression of the heart's longing for a greater intimacy with Him. It is to set aside our physical appetites and the time required to prepare meals in order to focus more of our time and attention on the Lord.

God's Promise

Perhaps the greatest Scripture on the subject of fasting is found in the wonderful passage in 2 Chronicles 7:14. This promise was given to Solomon in response to his prayer at the dedication of the Temple. The Word tells us that Solomon humbled himself before God, knelt down before all the congregation of Israel and spread his hands toward the heavens and began to pray. In his prayer in 2 Chronicles, chapter six, Solomon petitioned God that His eyes would be continually upon the Temple

> Fasting must be, first and foremost, an expression of the heart's longing for a greater intimacy with Him.

and that He would hear and forgive. Solomon prayed, *"...
hear thou from thy dwelling place, even from heaven; and
when thou hearest, forgive." (2 Chronicles 6:21).*

Solomon interceded on behalf of the children of
Israel and asked that whenever they were defeated before
their enemies or the heavens were shut up and there was no
rain because they had sinned against Him that He would
hear their prayers and forgive them. (See 2 Chronicles
6:22-27) He pleaded, *"...if they pray toward this place,
and confess thy name, and turn from their sin, when
thou dost afflict them; Then hear thou from heaven, and
forgive the sin of thy servants, and of thy people Israel..."*
(2 Chronicles 6:26-27).

God answered Solomon's prayer with an awesome
manifestation of His power. He sent down fire from
heaven to consume the burnt offering and sacrifices and
His glory filled the Temple to such a great extent that the
priests could not even enter. When the children of Israel
saw the fire and glory of God come down, they fell on
their faces and worshipped God.

Four Things God Requires of His People Today

Later in chapter seven we read about Solomon's divine encounter when God appeared to him and said, *"I have heard thy prayer, and have chosen this place to myself for an house of sacrifice" (2 Chronicles 7:12)*. He then gave the wonderful promise in 2 Chronicles 7:14 that the Church claims today, *"If my people, which are called by my name, shall humble themselves and pray, and seek my face, and turn from their wicked ways: then will I hear from heaven and will forgive their sin and will heal their land."*

Within this promise there are four things God requires of us:

- To humble ourselves.

- Pray.

- Seek His Face.

- Repent (turn from our wicked ways).

In the Church we have quoted and claimed God's promise of 2 Chronicles 7:14 when calling people to set aside designated times of prayer and fasting for our cities and nations. And, whenever these four conditions have been met, God has answered our prayers and we have experienced spiritual breakthroughs.

A City Transformed Through Prayer and Fasting

A powerful example of God's faithfulness in fulfilling this promise is the story of the city of Manchester, Kentucky in the documentary, "An Appalachian Dawn" produced by George Otis, Jr. and released by the Sentinel Group in October, 2010. This documentary highlights the transformation of the town of Manchester, located in Clay County, notorious for drug abuse, political corruption and crushing poverty.

Located in the heartland of Appalachia, the city of Manchester, Kentucky appeared to be the most unlikely place for societal breakthrough to occur. Any attempt to change the dysfunctional way of life was considered futile. With the decline of the coal and salt industries, a 1964 CBS news report gave Manchester the title of "Depressed City, USA."

Forty years later, Clay County could not escape from its backward stereotype and was listed as the sixth poorest county in the United States. In 2001, the Drug Enforcement Agency included Manchester in a region listed as the "Painkiller Capital of America."

Transformation Began with Prayers of Repentance

The community had lost all hope. Then, on May 2, 2004, 63 churches and 3,500 people united together. Church leaders publicly repented before God for their lack of civic involvement and the community united in a march against drugs. Many people felt this climactic prayer event helped break the vice-like grip of drug addition that had tormented their daily life.

The following year:

• Manchester became the only area in the region where painkiller prescriptions actually decreased!

• Drug arrests increased by 300 percent!

Soon government corruption was uncovered

and within three years, public officials, including the Mayor, City Supervisor, Assistant Police Chief, the 911 Director, Fire Chief, Circuit Court Judge, a handful of City Councilmen, County Commissioners and County Clerks, were exposed and jailed for racketeering, distributing drugs and voter fraud. Churches and citizens worked together with the law enforcement to root out this crime and corruption.

A court watch program was initiated by the churches, and with the help of their Congressman, a local Jesus-based rehabilitation center was completed in 2008.

Local drug dealers soon began surrendering their lives to Jesus and were getting delivered from drug addiction.

High ranking officials like the new Mayor and Sheriff began advancing the Kingdom cause of Christ in their spheres of influence.

As They Prayed and Fasted, God Turned It Around!

Here are just a few more of the major changes that resulted as the people humbled themselves, prayed and repented:

• Manchester was transformed through the power of prayer! From being a city where the people had lost all hope, In 2007, the city council voted to change the name of the city to "Manchester: City of Hope."

• Not only are students now being drug tested in school, Bible elective courses are also being offered in high school.

• Clay County was chosen as having the model-reading program in the state in 2008, which is very significant for a region traditionally plagued with high illiteracy rates.

• In the Fall of 2009, the city announced a recycling company would be coming to Manchester, bringing 1,400 new jobs; this despite the global recession.

• Clay County now possesses one of the largest Rocky

Mountain Elk populations in the country; and with turkey, bear, and deer populations making a comeback, a new campground and new bike trail accent a tourist industry on the upswing.

• Manchester city water was chosen in 2008 as having the best tasting water in a statewide competition. The local water treatment plant is now selling "Hope Water" as a commercial product.

What a tremendous testimony to the faithfulness of God in response to the united prayers of His people! This is just one example of what God will do when we humble ourselves before Him through fasting and prayer.

Humility and Repentance Moves the Hand of God!

Humility is a major aspect of fasting and positions us to be heard and to receive what we need from God. Mahesh Chavda, Senior Pastor of All Nations Church in Charlotte, North Carolina and Atlanta, Georgia. is a major Christian leader, especially in the area of intercession. He has gone on two 40-day water fasts a year for ten years.

As a result, the Lord has released unusual miracles in his ministry. In his book, *"The Hidden Power of Prayer and Fasting"* Chavda emphasizes the importance of humility positioning the Church for triumph. During a 40-day fast, God revealed to him that a worldwide revival was coming and that it would bring an unprecedented harvest of souls and glory to the earth. He states:

> The rains of the Holy Spirit are coming upon His last day church as never before! I believe that God is releasing the power again like He did at Azusa street. A fresh Pentecost is coming, a hundred-year bloom! Yet the Church can only begin to operate in the power of the Spirit when its members obtain the grace of God in their lives. How do we obtain grace? We humble ourselves. Proverbs 3:34 tells us that God "...gives grace to the humble."[3]

The Scriptural way of humbling yourself before God is through fasting described by King David in the Psalms. He said, *"...I humbled my soul with fasting..." (Psalm 35:13)*, "...When I wept and chastened my soul with fasting, that became my reproach (Psalm 69:10).

Throughout the Old Testament we see God's mercy

revealed upon all those who humbled themselves through fasting. The city of Ninevah was spared because the people humbled themselves in fasting and prayer. *"So the people of Ninevah believed God, and proclaimed a fast, and put on sackcloth, from the greatest of them even to the least of them" (Jonah 3:5).* Even the animals fasted! The people believed God! The King made a decree calling for everyone to turn from their evil ways, to stop the violence and to cry out to God for mercy. The Word says God saw their works that they turned from their evil ways and *"repented of the evil, that he had said that he would do unto them; and he did it not" (Jonah 3:10).*

Humility is a major aspect of fasting and positions you to be heard and to receive what you need from God.

King Ahab was the worst king that ever reigned over the northern kingdom of Israel. *"Surely there was no one like Ahab who sold himself to do evil in the sight of the LORD, because Jezebel his wife incited him (1 Kings 21:25).* Yet, when God proclaimed judgment against him through Elijah, Ahab *"tore his clothes and put on sackcloth and fasted, and lay in sackcloth, and went softly" (1 Kings 21:27).*

When God saw that Ahab humbled himself, the word of the LORD came to Elijah. God said, *"Have you noticed how Ahab has humbled himself before me? Because he has humbled himself, I will not bring this disaster in his day, but I will bring it on his house in the days of his son"* *(1 Kings 21:29, NIV).*

If fasting can move God to mercy on behalf of a wicked king like Ahab, think about how fasting can be used to have mercy upon us today when we humble ourselves before the Throne of Grace!

We Must Cast Off the Shackles of Pride

If we are going to see God's power manifested and our cities and nations transformed, Pastors, Ministers, Christian leaders, we must lead the way! We must be willing to get rid of our pride and humble ourselves before God's people and lead them in repenting for the sins we have allowed into the Church, as well as repent for the sins committed in our cities and nations!

One of the major sins hindering the Church from experiencing the release of God's power is pride. Peter wrote *"...be clothed with humility, for "God resisteth the proud, but giveth grace to the humble." Humble yourselves therefore under the mighty hand of God, that He may exalt you in due time" (1 Peter 5:5-6).*

There are many ministers who are so bound by spirits of pride and self-righteousness they are fearful that if they humble themselves before God in confessing and repenting for the sins that have entered the church, and lead their people in prayers of repentance, they will somehow lose their position of influence or standing with the people.

If we allow it to gain a stronghold in our lives, pride will hinder our intimacy with God and block us from receiving what we need because God resists the proud. However, when we humble ourselves through fasting, we break the chains of pride off our lives and receive God's grace and power! God is calling His people...you and me...to humble ourselves individually and corporately through fasting, seek His face and turn from OUR wicked ways and repent. In response, He will hear us. He will forgive OUR sins, and He will heal OUR lands.

When you humble yourself through fasting, confess and repent of any and all sins and failures. Like David, cry out to God, *"Search me, O God, and know my heart: try me, and know my thoughts: And see if there be any wicked way in me, and lead me in the way everlasting"* (Psalm 139:23-24).

Fasting is a means of bringing the flesh into submission to the Lord so He can strengthen and deliver us from harmful habits and overcome the works of our flesh. If there are habits, unconfessed sins, unforgiveness, bitterness, lust, or worldly desires that are weighing you down and hindering the flow of God's power and anointing in your life, as you confess them God will give you His grace to overcome.

Ezra's Humility Through Fasting and Prayer Brought Revival!

Consider Ezra's humility and brokenness when he learned that the priests and Levites had not separated themselves from the people of the lands and had committed the abominations of the Canaanites, Hittites, Perizzites, Jebusites, Ammonites, Moabites, Egyptians and Amorites.

> Fasting is a means of bringing the flesh into submission to the Lord.

(See Ezra 9:1-2) When he heard this he tore his garment and mantle, plucked off hair from his head and beard and sat down appalled until the evening sacrifice. Then, at the evening sacrifice, he rose from his humiliation with his torn garments fell on his knees with his hands outstretched to God and prayed.

Ezra cried out to God:

"O my God, I am ashamed and blush to lift up my face to thee, my God: for our iniquities are increased over our head, and our trespass is grown up into the heavens" (Ezra 9:6).

How long has it been since we have seen this type of humility and brokenness in our pulpits over the sin that permeates our cities and nations?

Pastors, how long has it been since you have wept, humbled yourself through fasting and prayed over the sin that has infiltrated the Church?

Ezra was a Priest and Scribe in the Law of Moses, *"...well versed in the Law of Moses, which the LORD, the God of Israel, had given"* (Ezra 7:6, NIV). He was a righteous man who loved God and had determined in his heart to observe and teach the Law of the LORD and its decrees to the people, *"For Ezra had devoted himself to the study and observance of the Law of the LORD, and to teaching its decrees and laws in Israel" (Ezra 7:10, NIV).*

Notice in Ezra's intercession before God on behalf of the people, he did not point an accusing finger at them and say "Oh God, look at these evil people and the great sins they have committed." He identified with them and their sins by saying "our iniquities" and "our trespass." Ezra's prayer is a tremendous example of what it means to stand in the gap for others through intercession. It reveals the type of humility we must have when we come before God in prayer and fasting for our cities and nations.

> Pastors, how long has it been since you have wept, humbled yourself through fasting and prayed over the sin that has infiltrated the Church?

Ezra's humility through fasting and prayer was used by God to bring about a great revival and reformation in Israel! When the people saw Ezra bowed down on His face before the house of God, they all came together in a *"very great assembly of men, women and children" (Ezra 10:1).* The people wept bitterly and repented of their sins, made a covenant with God to put away all their foreign wives and children, and each one guilty of marrying foreign wives offered a trespass offering.

Church, We Must Lead the Way!

Here in America, we must take upon ourselves the burden and say, "Oh God, we have sinned! We have done wickedly. In America and in our cities, we have turned away from you. We have pushed you out of our schools and out of our government. We have allowed the murder of millions of innocent unborn babies. We have rejected your Word and have condoned and promoted the sins of promiscuousness, homosexuality, lust, perversion, pornography, prostitution, immorality, adultery, and fornication. As a nation, we have sinned and are filled with greed, selfishness and materialism. We have forgotten you and are puffed up with pride in our accomplishments as a nation thinking it is by our own power and might we have become a strong and mighty nation. Forgive us, O LORD! Look down upon us in your great love and mercy. Restore the faith of our fathers and make us once again a righteous nation built upon the foundation of Your Word. Not for our sakes but for Your great Name's sake! Forgive us our sins and heal our land!"

Humility and True 'Heart' Repentance Bring Revival!

Humility and repentance during our times of fasting and prayer are the keys to experiencing personal and corporate revival! As I mentioned in chapter one, God is calling His people—the Church—to seasons of fasting and prayer. Hear the cry of the Spirit:

"...Turn ye even to me with all your heart, and with fasting, and with weeping, and with mourning: And rend your heart, and not your garments, and turn unto the LORD your God: for he is gracious and merciful, slow to anger, and of great kindness, and repenteth him of the evil" (Joel 2:12-13).

In these verses there are three actions God is asking you to take:

1. Turn to Him with all your heart.

2. Rend your heart.

3. Repent.

It is not just the outward observance of fasting that God is looking for. The fasting that God honors is the fast that begins with the attitude of the heart. The word *"rend"* in Hebrew is *"qara'"* meaning "to tear, to rend away". Although the outward observance of fasting in the Old Testament was the tearing of their garments as a sign of great grief for their sins, instead of just rending their garments, God was requiring them to rend their hearts.

God isn't looking just for the outward expression; He requires the rending of our hearts. The outward observance of fasting is just a mockery and affront to God if it isn't accompanied by a broken and contrite spirit. *"The sacrifices of God are a broken spirit: a broken and a contrite heart, O God, thou will not despise" (Psalm 51:17)*. When we are genuinely grieved in our hearts for sin and earnestly desire to turn from them, then God will hear us and answer.

What is the Fast That is Pleasing to God?

As you fast, ask yourself, "Am I really seeking God with all my heart, or am I just going through the motions?" Humble yourself before God and allow Him to reveal any sin, disobedience, wrong attitude, habit or worldly desire that is displeasing to Him. Allow your heart to be broken before God with a genuine godly sorrow for your sin. Then, from your heart confess, repent and turn from your sin. God will pour out His love and mercy in forgiveness and deliver you!

It is possible to go through all the outward actions of fasting but fail to make a divine connection with the power and presence of Almighty God due to wrong motives. When you fast, if your major motive isn't to draw closer to God and know Him in a deeper, more intimate relationship, you shouldn't begin the fast.

There was a time when God spoke to the children of Israel and the priests and told them although they had gone through the outward motions of fasting that He would not hear them. God did not accept their fast days nor answer their prayers during their 70 years of captivity because when they fasted, they were really not fasting unto Him. They asked God, *"Why*

> The outward observance of fasting is just a mockery and affront to God if it isn't accompanied by a broken and contrite spirit.

have we fasted...and you have not seen it? Why have we humbled ourselves, and you have not noticed?" (Isaiah 58:3, NIV)

God spoke through the prophet Zechariah saying, *"When ye fasted and mourned in the fifth and seventh month, even those seventy years, did ye at all fast unto me, even unto me? (Zechariah 7:5).*

What a soul-searching question! Search your heart and ask yourself, "When I fast, am I really fasting unto God?"

What type of fast is pleasing to God? In Chapter four we will consider the motives and actions God requires as we fast unto Him.

.

FASTING
THAT MOVES
GOD'S HAND

Chapter Four

The Fasting that God Accepts

"Is not this the fast that I have chosen ? to loose the bands
of wickedness, to undo the heavy burdens, and to let the
oppressed go free, and that ye break every yoke?"
Isaiah 58:6

The Fasting that God Accepts

One of the most important things you need to consider when beginning a fast is your motive. You need to look deep into your heart and ask yourself, "What is my real motive for entering this fast? "Am I really fasting unto God?

Too often in the Church we concentrate on the method or strategies used in fasting and give very little thought concerning our motives and the attitudes of our hearts.

In previous chapters we have looked at what true Biblical fasting involves and have learned:

- True Biblical fasting is much more than a religious exercise.

- It is more than an act of self-denial.

- It is not a manipulative tool to get something from God.

- We do not fast to earn something from God, but to make a divine connection with Him.

- Fasting is not just a spiritual discipline for bringing problems to God to be fixed.

- Fasting must be first and foremost an expression of the heart's longing for a greater intimacy with Him.

- Fasting involves true humility and repentance.

In this chapter I want us to consider the motives and attitudes of our hearts that are so important to God when we fast and the type of fast that pleases Him. God isn't as concerned about the outward observance of fasting as He is with our hearts.

If our fasting is to be acceptable to Him, our motives must first be pure resulting in a life that is dedicated and committed to Him. We cannot expect our fasting to move God's hand on our behalf or on behalf of our cities or nations, if our hearts are not right before Him and if we are not living in accordance with His Word.

We are going to look at the lives of two men that were greatly used by God, through their prayer and fasting, to move God's hand on behalf of Israel: Daniel and Moses. As we do, I want you to realize that what God did for them He will do for you. Many Christians look at these great "spiritual giants" and how God used them so mightily and think, "I could never be used by God the way they were." But they are wrong! God can and will use your prayers and fasting to move God's hand on behalf of your family, city and nation if you are willing, obedient and you are fasting according to God's purposes in a way that is pleasing to Him.

> God isn't as concerned about the outward observance of fasting as He is with our hearts.

Don't Get Hung Up!

The fast that pleases God and moves His hand isn't dependent on the length or extent of your fast. He isn't impressed with how many days you fast. Whether you fast three days, twenty-one days, forty days or just one day isn't the most important thing. Neither does He consider the person that fasts forty days more spiritual or stronger than the one that fasts a shorter period of time.

In his book, *The Rewards of Fasting*, Mike Bickle, founder and director of the International House of Prayer in Kansas City states:

> We will sustain a life of fasting only by God's grace, not by our own strength.

> Fasting is more than gritting our teeth as we endure it. Instead, we ask God for grace to enter into the mystery of connecting with Him in fasting. As we embrace the voluntary weakness of fasting, we receive more spiritual strength in our walk with God. His grace multiplies to those who pursue it.[1]

When you fast, don't get hung up on the number of days you fast, or try to fast in your own strength. Be led by His Spirit and draw upon the strength of the Lord. I don't believe that Moses, Elijah, Daniel, or most of the other saints in the Bible who fasted, had a predetermined, set amount of days they were going to fast. Their major motive was to connect with God.

Daniel's Prayer and Fasting Moved the Hand of God

In Daniel, chapter nine when Daniel understood prophetically God's timing when Israel's desolation would be over and God would deliver the children of Israel out of captivity, he said, *"I set my face unto the Lord God, to seek by prayer and supplications, with fasting, and sackcloth and ashes" (Daniel 9:3).* Based upon God's promise that He would deliver the children of Israel out of their captivity, bring them back to their land, and restore their temple, houses and lands, Daniel determined to take hold of that promise through prayer and fasting.

Daniel knew that the current year was the year when the seventy years of captivity would end, but the decree for their release was not yet issued. That is why he determined to fast and pray until He touched the heart of God and moved His hand on behalf of the children of Israel.

Daniel didn't set a predetermined amount of days for his fast. He didn't enter his fast thinking, "I'm going to fast a week, ten days or twenty-one days. He was determined, persistent and focused! He had a spiritual goal. He didn't know how long it would take, but I believe he determined in his heart he was going to humble himself through fasting to seek God's face until He heard from God.

This is the heart attitude you must have when you fast. You must set your spiritual focus like Daniel did upon whatever need, promise or prophetic word that has been spoken over your life. Determine in your heart to humble yourself through fasting, regardless of how long it may take, until you hear from God.

The Fasting that Moves God's Hand Begins with the Attitude of Our Hearts

Once again we see that the fast that moves God's hand begins with the attitude of the heart. It involves humbling ourselves before God, having a genuine sorrow for our sins, having a repentant heart and a willingness to turn from our own ways and everything that is displeasing to God.

In Daniel's prayer we see his humility as he confessed and repented on behalf of Israel's sins. He said, *"We have sinned...we have rebelled."* He confessed, *"O LORD, we and our kings, our princes and our fathers are covered with shame because we have sinned against you. The Lord our God is merciful and forgiving, even though we have rebelled against him..."* *(Daniel 9:8-9, NIV).*

> The fast that moves God's hand requires humility, genuine sorrow for our sins, a repentant heart and a willingness to turn from all sin and everything displeasing to God.

He didn't try to make excuses for their sins or make his plea based upon any goodness in himself or the people of Israel. He pled for God's mercy saying, *"for we do not present our supplications before thee for our righteousness, but for thy great mercies"* *(Daniel 9:18).*

One of the things missing today is a sense of shame for the sins that are being committed around us in our cities and nations. The Church has sat silently by and watched sin increase and penetrate every area of our society. We have not only failed to speak out and take a stand against sins that are being flaunted in our faces, but there is no shame or remorse for the sins that have infiltrated the Church.

God help us!

As Daniel Fasted and Prayed, God's Prophetic Promise was Fulfilled!

We don't know how long Daniel prayed or fasted in this instance, but the Word says that while He was still speaking, praying and confessing, his prayer reached the heavens and moved the hand of God. God saw Daniel's heart, heard his prayer and issued the command, dispatching Gabriel to bring Daniel revelation concerning the timing of the deliverance of the children of Israel from their 70 years of captivity. Gabriel told Daniel, *"At the beginning of thy supplications the commandment came forth, and I am come to shew thee..." (Daniel 9:23).*

God heard Daniel's prayer and fulfilled His promise. He moved on the heart of Cyrus, king of Persia, to make a decree throughout his kingdom that the people of Israel could return to Israel and rebuild Jerusalem. There were 72,332 Israelites, along with 7,337 of their servants, who returned to Israel with wealth and riches and a freewill offering for the temple in Jerusalem!

What are the prophecies and promises that God has given you for your personal life and ministry?

What are the prophecies that God has spoken over your city and nation?

Set your heart and mind to seek God's face, to fast and pray like Daniel, until you receive the confirmation in your spirit that God has heard you, and the answer is on its way.

As He Fasted, Moses Touched God and Revelation Came!

When God called Moses to come up to Mount Sinai to meet with him, Moses had not predetermined in his heart that he would be fasting forty days and nights on the mountain. His heart was focused on communing with God. In his hunger to know God intimately, his needs and natural desires were laid aside… forgotten. Moses said, *"I neither did eat bread nor drink water:"* *(Deuteronomy 9:9).* He prostrated himself before God. His heart and mind were focused solely upon God and he was one-hundred percent submitted to Him.

> The question during fasting is not will God meet with you and meet your needs; but, rather, are you willing to fast and pray until you have a greater revelation of Him?

Those forty days Moses spent in the awesome Presence of God was a holy, sacred time. Moses was lifted into a high spiritual realm where his spirit was in direct communion with God. In that holy atmosphere—Moses touched God and revelation came! God not only revealed Himself to Moses, He also revealed His plan for Israel and gave him laws and commandments for them to follow.

How hungry—how desperate are you for God's presence? God is calling us, as He did Moses, to meet with Him. He is calling us up to the mountain of God where we will enter His presence and present ourselves to Him so that He can reveal more of Himself to us.

The question during fasting is not will God meet with you and meet your needs; but rather, are you willing to set yourself apart in fasting and prayer until you have a greater revelation of Him?

Through His Prayer and Fasting Moses Moved the Hand of God to Spare Israel

In Deuteronomy 10 we read how that a second time Moses prostrated himself before the Lord in 40 days of fasting and prayer. During this fast, Moses stood in the gap for Israel. God was ready to destroy the children of Israel because they had committed spiritual adultery in building a golden calf and worshipping it. He told Moses, *"...let me alone, that my wrath may wax hot against them, and that I may consume them: and I will make of thee a great nation" (Exodus 32:10).*

God knew the power of Moses' intercession and that he would prevail in prayer on their behalf, so He said, "Let me alone!"

Do you see the power God has given you through prayer and fasting whereby you can prevail with God for nations?

Moses did not let go of God! He did not let Him alone! He poured out his life in intercession. There on the mountain Moses cried out and interceded before God on Israel's behalf. He said, *"And I fell down before the LORD, as at the first, forty days and forty nights: I did neither eat bread, nor drink water...For I was afraid of the anger and hot displeasure, wherewith the LORD was wroth against you to destroy you" (Deuteronomy 9:18-19).*

It was a matter of life and death for the children of Israel! Moses pursued God during that second forty-day period on Mt. Sinai. His personal needs, interests and desires were all laid aside as he cried out and interceded before God on Israel's behalf. Through his prayer and fasting, He moved the hand of God. God granted Moses' petition and spared the people. Moses said, *"But the Lord hearkened unto me at that time also" (Deuteronomy 9:19).*

When You Fast, It Must Be Unto God

Moses' prayer and fasting moved God's hand on behalf of Israel not because of the length of his fast but because his heart and motives were pure. There is no spiritual benefit to be gained simply by abstaining from eating. Let me stress this point again: we do not earn God's favor or blessings through our good works or self-denial. And, we must guard against the danger of our fasting becoming legalistic.

It is not the self-denial and the bringing of the fleshly appetite into submission that is so important and moves the hand of God. When you fast, it must be unto God. Jesus said when you fast "... *unto thy Father which is in secret: and thy Father, which seeth in secret, shall reward thee openly" (Matthew 6:18)*. Fasting is between you and the Father, and there is a reward waiting for you...for all those who shut themselves away in the secret place of fasting and prayer.

> When you fast with the right motives, you set in motion God's power to work on your behalf.

Whenever you respond to God's call to fast with the right motives and according to His plan and purposes, you set in motion the miraculous power of God to work on your behalf!

Fasting God Refuses to Accept

As the Old Testament period came to a close, the spiritual discipline of fasting had become a legalistic obligation which had lost both its meaning to the individual and its effectiveness before God.

God spoke to the children of Israel and the priests and told them that although they had gone through the outward motions of fasting that He would not hear them because their motives were wrong and they had refused to hear and obey Him. During their 70 years of captivity, God refused to accept their fast days and answer their prayers because they were not really fasting unto Him.

God told Zechariah, "Speak unto all the people of the land, and to the priests, saying, When ye fasted and mourned in the fifth and seventh month, even those seventy years, did ye at all fast unto me, even unto me?" (Zechariah 7:5). While they religiously observed the fast days, they "refused to hearken, and pulled away the shoulder, and stopped their ears, that they should not hear" (Zechariah 7:11)

Their fasting was not accepted by God because their motives were wrong. Their hearts were far from Him and they were just going through a religious exercise. They hardened their hearts and refused to *"hear the law, and the words which the Lord, of hosts hath sent in his spirit by the former prophets" (Zechariah 7:12).*

The fast that is pleasing to God and moves His hand is not based solely on the outward observance of fasting—abstaining from food for a specified period of time. The children of Israel were outwardly righteous and observed the designated fasting days but they were not living according to the ordinances God had established. As a result, God refused to hear them. He said, *"...so they cried, and I would not hear, saith the LORD of hosts" (Zechariah 7:13).*

It's Time to Boldly Cry Out—To Expose Sin and Call for Repentance

In Isaiah, chapter 58, God has made it clear concerning the type of fast that is pleasing to Him and to which He responds. He begins by instructing the prophet Isaiah to boldly show and convince the people of their sins. He was not to coddle them or sugar coat the truth.

He must not worry about whether or not it would offend them or cause them to reject him and his message. God told him to *"CRY aloud, spare not, lift up thy voice like a trumpet, and shew my people their transgression, and the house of Jacob their sins" (Isaiah 58:1).*

Pastors, ministers, evangelists, church leaders, the call to us today is just as clear as it was to Isaiah. If we truly want to see God's power and glory manifested in our churches and our cities transformed, we must not hold back for fear of hurting the people's feelings or care about what others may think. You must cry as loud as you can! Our responsibility before God is to boldly and fearlessly expose sin and call for repentance!

Hypocritical Fasting Exposed!

Before revealing the type of fast that is pleasing to Him, God exposed the hypocrisy of the people and clearly showed them the type of fast that is unacceptable. To all outward appearances, the people were walking in obedience and were serving Him. God said, *"For day after day they seek me out; they seem eager to know my ways, as if they were a nation that does what is right and has not forsaken the commands of its God" (Isaiah 58:2, NIV).*

They were going through the forms and rituals, but they continued in their sins. They were puffed up with pride and asked God, *"Why have we fasted...and you have not seen it?" (Isaiah 58:3, NIV)* Their eyes were blinded from seeing their true condition and they were pointing their fingers at God because He had not answered them.

The reason why their fast was not acceptable to God?

They had not fasted *unto* Him.

They fasted, but they persisted in their sins and did not turn from their evil ways. God told them that although they had fasted, *"on the day of your fasting, you do as you please and exploit all your workers. Your fasting ends in quarreling and strife, and in striking each other with wicked fists. You cannot fast as you do today and expect your voice to be heard on high" (Isaiah 58:3-4, NIV).*

1. The people fasted but they continued to do their own pleasures—whatever seemed right in their own eyes—whether it was lawful or unlawful. Though it appeared outwardly that they afflicted their souls, they still gratified the lusts of their flesh and made them their law.

2. They were contentious and spiteful. On a day when they should be grieving for their sins, they were hard taskmasters and exploited their workers.

3. They fasted for strife. Instead of judging themselves, they condemned one another which ended in striking one another with their fists.

As long as they continued in their sins, their outward observance of their fasting was an affront to God. Their fasting and prayer was nothing more than empty words and actions. What we learn from this passage of Scripture is that it is not enough to just go through the motions of fasting, while there is still sin in our lives that we refuse to acknowledge, confess and turn away from. That is hypocrisy and actually is an abomination to God.

The fast that pleases God involves more than just afflicting our souls by abstaining from food for a period of time. We must develop a fasted lifestyle where our days of fasting and prayer are accompanied by righteous acts and righteous living through the power of the Holy Spirit.

God's Chosen Fast

After revealing the type of fast that is not acceptable to Him, God outlines for us the type of fast that pleases Him and the blessings we will receive as a result. He said, *"Is not this the fast that I have chosen? To loose the bands of wickedness, to undo the heavy burdens, and to let the oppressed go free, and that ye break every yoke? Is it not to deal thy bread to the hungry, and that thou bring the poor that are cast out to thy house? When thou seest the naked, that thou cover him; and that thou hide not thyself from thine own flesh?" (Isaiah 58:6-7).*

In these verses we see clearly that God does not intend fasting to be simply a religious act for us to observe. He expects us to also be walking in obedience to Him and ministering to the needs of others. He wants to use us to break the yoke of bondages that are upon people in our neighborhoods, on the job, at the marketplace and everywhere we go.

Fasting God's way is a means of bringing us into a powerful spiritual dimension where the faith that moves mountains is released into our lives, and our prayers become powerful and mighty to the pulling down of strongholds.

The purposes of God's chosen fast are:

1. To loose the bands or chains of wickedness.

2. To undo the heavy burdens.

3. To let the oppressed go free.

4. To break every yoke.

As we fast, God directs us to:

5. Share our food with the hungry.

6.   Provide shelter for the homeless.

7.   Provide clothing for those who have none.

8.   Do Not hide ourselves from the needs of our own flesh and blood.

A Yoke-Breaking Anointing is Released When We Fast and Pray!

The major purpose of God's chosen fast is to loose bonds of wickedness, undo heavy burdens, to set captives free and to break every yoke! The word "yoke" in verse six is derived from the Hebrew word, "hfom" which referred to the bars of the yoke. The literal yoke was a piece of timber or a heavy wooden pole, shaped to fit over the neck with curved pieces of wood around the neck fastened to the pole. The yoke was held in place on the animal by leather bands. The yoke was used to hitch together a team of animals, allowing them to be attached to a plow or a cart and to pull the load evenly.

The yoke refers to any burden, obligation or hardship

166

imposed or borne by another. It is something that binds, that keeps us burdened down, and that hinders people from walking in total freedom and from walking in the fullness of God's blessings. Yokes hinder Christians from rising up to reach their full spiritual potential in Christ.

Sickness, disease, and physical handicaps are yokes of bondage!

Lack of finances, debt, and poverty are yokes of bondage!

Nicotine, drugs, alcohol and other harmful habits are yokes of bondage!

Family turmoil, broken family relationships and marital problems are yokes of bondage!

Regardless of the yoke of bondage you may be struggling under; whether it is physical illness, major financial problems, a family member bound by drugs or alcohol, the breakup of your marriage, the loss of your job or home, as you fast and pray God will turn the battle around!

There are yokes of bondages in our cities and nations that can only be broken through fasting and prayer! We must reach out to the homeless living on our streets, help provide shelter and clothing, and feed the needy. Not only must we fast and pray, God wants to use us to help break the yokes of bondage off people in His Name!

> Not only must we fast and pray, God wants to use us to help break the yokes of bondage off people in His Name!

In Isaiah 10:27 we read, *"And it shall come to pass in that day, that his burden shall be taken away from off thy shoulder, and his yoke from off thy neck, and the yoke shall be destroyed because of the anointing."*

There is a yoke breaking anointing released when we fast and pray! There are circumstances and situations in our lives, and in the lives of people we see on a daily basis, that can only be remedied through the anointing of the Holy Spirit.

As you fast unto God, not only will He break every yoke of bondage off your life, He will release His anointing and use you to break the yokes of bondage off people around you who are bound by sin, addictions, physical infirmities, financial burdens and who are burdened and oppressed by the enemy.

There is a yoke breaking anointing released when you fast and pray!

Get ready for God to break through the barriers the enemy has built and receive the answers to the prayers you have been praying for years—holding on to God and believing Him for an answer!

Yokes of Sickness and Financial Bondage Broken Through Fasting

Jentezen Franklin, Pastor of the Free Chapel Church in Gainesville, Georgia begins each year by leading his church in a 21-Day fast. In his breakthrough book, *Fasting*, he shares the following awesome testimony how that God broke the yokes of sickness and financial bondage off a woman and her son as she joined in one of their 21-Day fasts.

Lisa and her son, Ben, used to attend Free Chapel. Life came to a jolting halt for them at one point after Ben was diagnosed with leukemia. He had gone through chemotherapy and had all the side effects, On January 5, the first Sunday in January when we began the fast, Ben was lying in the Intensive Care Unit, literally fighting for his life with a 107-degree fever. I knew the severity of the situation, so I proclaimed that we would begin that fast for Ben's recovery. Lisa told me Ben awoke at that same moment—the fever broke, he suffered no brain damage, and the leukemia went into total remission.

But Lisa's story doesn't stop there. She joined the twenty-one day fast that year and continued on it for a full forty days. This mother, in financial crisis, with a son near death and suffering from leukemia fasted for forty days. God honors that kind of faith and devotion. The Holy Spirit spoke to a man and his wife in our church to buy Lisa a brand new van. I called her and asked if she could come by the church office, but I didn't tell her anything further. On her way, the car she was driving at the time broke down! She finally arrived, terribly apologetic, having no idea what was about to happen. I handed her the keys to a beautiful new van complete with a DVD player for Ben to enjoy—and a check for an extra five thousand dollars that the couple wanted her to have!

Several weeks later, I called her up on the platform, and we shared her testimony.

Earlier that morning, I asked her how much debt she was in. She said she only owed twenty thousand dollars on her house because she had paid off all her other debts with the prior five-thousand-dollar gift. In that morning service, I presented her with another check from that same couple, this time for twenty-five thousand dollars. Lisa and her son had lived their last year in poverty, thanks to a debt-free future, the open reward that God poured out on their sacrificial obedience.[2]

10 Major Blessings God Has Promised to Those Who Choose to Fast His Way

In Isaiah, verses 6-7 God instructs us concerning the type of fast He is pleased with and what He expects us to do. In the following verse He then reveals His promised

blessings to those who follow His chosen fast.

As you fast, expect these 10 major blessings to be released in your life!

In his book, *Revival Now Through Prayer and Fasting*, Gordon Cove points out the fact that in Isaiah 58 God gives His people a right and a wrong reason to fast. He states:

> Having shown them where they were wrong, He proceeds to give them instructions and promises regarding the right way to fast. So that all the promises mentioned here are conditional upon us exercising the correct method of fasting. These promises begin at verse eight.

> The first word of the verse is 'Then.' This means, 'at that time,' or 'after something else has happened.' It is only when we are practicing the fast that God has chosen, that we can claim the promises. Not until then.[3]

There are at least 10 major blessings in Isaiah 58 you

172

can expect in your life as you fast with the right motives and according to God's purposes.

1. **Revelation.** God promises, *"Then your light will break forth like the dawn..."* (verse 8, NIV).

2. **Healing and wholeness.** *God promises, "your healing will quickly appear"* (verse 8, NIV).

3. **Righteousness.** *God promises, "your righteousness shall go before you"* (verse 8, NIV).

4. **God's presence and glory.** God promises, *"the glory of the LORD will be your rear guard"* (verse 8, NIV).

5. **Answered prayers.** God promises, *"Then you will call, and the LORD will answer, you will cry for help, and he will say: Here am I"* (verse 9, NIV)

6. **Continual guidance.** God promises, *"The LORD will guide you always"* (verse 11, NIV).

7. **Contentment.** God promises, *"he will satisfy your needs in a sun-scorched land"* (Verse 11, NIV).

8. **Strength.** *God promises He will "strengthen your frame"* (verse 11, NIV).

9. **Continual supply.** God promises, *"You will be like a well-watered garden, like a spring whose waters never fail" (verse 11, NIV).*

10. **Restoration.** God promises, *"Your people will rebuild the ancient ruins and will raise up the age-old foundations; you will be called Repairer of Broken Walls, Restorer of Streets with Dwellings" (verse 12, NIV).*

All of these divine benefits and more are what you can expect in your life as you fast with the right motives and follow God's instructions concerning the fast He has chosen.

Fasting Enables You to Enter A New Powerful Spiritual Dimension

One of the greatest benefits of fasting is that it allows you to shut out the natural world and enter a powerful spiritual dimension where you experience a deeper level of communion and fellowship with God.

When we fast unto the Lord we are declaring our great need of Him. During this time, our spirits become more sensitive to the Holy Spirit, His leading and direction and we are able to hear His voice more clearly.

As we shut out worldly distractions and our natural desires and bring them into submission to the Spirit, we develop a greater hunger and thirst for spiritual nourishment that comes from the Word and being in God's presence.

One day the disciples came to Jesus and urged Him to eat after a long day's journey. While He ministered to the Samaritan woman at Jacob's well they had gone into the city to buy food. (See John 4:6-8) They had returned with the food and encouraged Him to eat. His reply was, *"I have food to eat that you know nothing about" (John 4:32, NIV)*. The disciples were puzzled and asked one another if someone had brought him something to eat while they were in the city buying food.

Jesus, seeing their confusion and lack of understanding said to them, *"My food...is to do the will of him who sent me and to finish his work" (John 4:34, NIV)*.

Jesus wanted them to know that there was something more than physical food that sustained Him. He was nourished and sustained through His communion with His Father and in doing His will. The more you develop a lifestyle of prayer and fasting, setting aside more and more time to fast and pray on a regular basis, your desire for God and doing His will will increase. Your dependence on the natural things of this world will diminish and you will be nourished and strengthened through your communion with Him.

> The more you develop a lifestyle of fasting, your desire for God and doing His will will increase in your life.

Jesus taught and demonstrated the importance of fasting. Before He began His ministry, He was led by the Spirit on a 40-Day fast where He went into the wilderness. When He went into the wilderness, He was "full of" the Holy Ghost (Luke 4:1), and when He left He wasn't weak or worn out. He returned in the "power of" the Holy Ghost! (Luke 4:14). One of the first things we read about that He did after His 40-Day fast was to cast a demon out of a man in the synagogue.

There are Christians who fail to see the importance of fasting because they think there is little teaching in the New Testament on the subject. They read the passage of Scripture in Matthew 9:14 where the disciples of John came to Jesus and asked, *"Why do we and the Pharisees fast oft, but thy disciples fast not?"* and think fasting was no longer emphasized. Jesus not only has taught us the importance of fasting and how to fast but also the power that is realized through fasting. In chapter five we will focus on what He taught and demonstrated about fasting.

The Anointing Breaks Every Yoke!

As you hear this call of God's Spirit to consecrate and set aside time to fast and pray on a regular basis, God's strength and power will be released into your life in a new dimension. Bondages will be broken in His mighty Name!

God has promised, *"And it shall come to pass that before they call, I will answer; and while they are yet speaking I will hear (Isaiah 65:34).* This is God's promise to you! He said even before you call, he will answer you. It is not His desire to withhold His blessings from you. He is not reluctant to meet your needs. He is already working on your behalf.

What is the heavy burden you have been carrying that has worn you down until you have become weary and discouraged? What are the circumstances in your life the enemy is using to attack and oppress your mind—to weaken your faith—to bring you to a point of complacency until you are no longer expecting and trusting God to manifest His power in your circumstances to meet your needs?

When Jesus saw the woman who had been bound with a spirit of infirmity for eighteen long years, He called her to Him, laid His hands on her and said, *"Woman, thou art loosed from thine infirmity" (Luke 13:12).* Jesus did not hesitate or wonder if it was God's will: He loosed her from her pain and suffering.

Now is your time to be set free from every physical infirmity—every financial burden—every hindrance—

every fear—every temptation—every habit—every obstacle that hinders you from taking hold of what God has provided for you. As you begin your fast, set your spiritual focus on God's promises to you, reach out in faith and receive whatever you need from Him.

FASTING
THAT MOVES
GOD'S HAND

Chapter Five

When ...Not "If"

"But thou, when thou fastest , anoint thine head,
and wash thy face; That thou appear not unto men to fast ,
but unto thy Father which is in secret: and thy Father, which
seeth in secret, shall reward thee openly."
Matthew 6:17-18

When ... Not "If!"

The importance of Biblical fasting in the life of every true disciple of Jesus Christ cannot be overemphasized. Fasting is not just a spiritual discipline reserved for great spiritual leaders or those in the fivefold ministry. It is an essential part of the life of every believer who truly desires to live in close communion and fellowship with God and is hungry to have His power manifested in their lives.

Due to a lack of teaching and emphasis in the Church, many Christians consider fasting to be something optional and feel that it isn't really necessary for them to fast. And while Jesus did not establish rules and regulations concerning fasting, He made it clear through His example and teaching that

> It is not a matter of "If" you should fast, but rather, "When" you fast.

every true disciple of His will fast. As we look closely at Jesus' teaching, you will clearly see that it is not a matter of "If" you should fast, but rather, "When" you fast.

Jesus Inaugurated His Ministry with a 40-Day Fast

We see the importance of fasting emphasized in the life of Jesus. Before He began His ministry, the first thing He did immediately following His baptism in the Jordan river was to go on a 40-day fast. Most often when we think about the 40 days Jesus spent in the wilderness, we often associate it with being a time of temptation. Many Christians have the idea that the main reason Jesus went into the wilderness was to be tempted of the devil. Jesus could have met the devil any place.

We know he was tempted during his 40 days in the wilderness. However, the Word is clear that Jesus was led by the Spirit into the wilderness. *"And Jesus being full of the Holy Ghost returned from Jordan, and was led by the Spirit into the wilderness. Being forty days tempted of the devil. And in those days he did eat nothing: and when they were ended, he afterward hungered"* (Luke 4:1-2).

I believe that the major purpose Jesus was led by the Spirit into the wilderness, where he fasted forty days, eating nothing, is that it was a time of spiritual preparation. It was a time of setting Himself apart to be alone with His Father. It was no doubt a time of focusing on the purpose for which He was sent into the world and a time of being strengthened. Instead of immediately returning to Galilee to begin the work God had sent Him to do of destroying the works of the devil, He went into the wilderness to fast and pray.

Why 40 Days?

Throughout Scripture, the number forty, like the number seven, has a special spiritual significance. It signifies a time of completeness.

- God caused it to rain forty days and nights in destroying the wicked from the earth with a flood. During that time God preserved Noah and a righteous remnant.

- Moses lived in the wilderness in Midian forty years before God appeared to him out of the burning bush and commissioned him to lead Israel out of bondage.

• Moses fasted forty days two times: when he met with God on Mt. Sinai and received the Ten Commandments and a second time after the children of Israel sinned and God was ready to destroy them because of their rebellion.

• The children of Israel wandered forty years in the wilderness until the time allotted by God to complete their punishment for their disobedience.

• Elijah fasted forty days and nights and was sustained by the supernatural provision of God.

During Jesus' forty-day fast, it was a time of completeness. He consecrated Himself and focused His heart and mind solely upon fulfilling God's will. He gave Himself wholly to God.

If Jesus, the Son of the living God, felt the need, and was directed by the Holy Spirit to set aside 40 days to consecrate and prepare Himself for the work God had given Him to do; how much more must we be willing to set aside seasons of prayer and fasting to fast consecrating ourselves to the work of God?

Following His 40-Day Fast, Jesus Returned in the Power of the Spirit!

When Jesus completed His forty-day fast He did not leave the wilderness in a worn out, weakened condition. In a careful study of the Scriptures, we see that after forty days of fasting, where He defeated Satan and overcame every temptation; angels were sent to minister to Him. (Matthew 4:11) Also notice that in Luke, chapter four, verse one, it says Jesus was *"full of"* the Holy Ghost when He entered His 40-day fast, and in verse 14 after He left the wilderness we read that Jesus returned *"in the power of the Spirit"*.

> The man who never fasts is no more on the way to heaven than the man who never prays.
> – John Wesley

At His baptism at the Jordan River, the Holy Spirit descended in the form of a dove and rested upon Jesus. *"Now when all the people were baptized, it came to pass, that Jesus also being baptized, and praying, the heaven was opened, and the Holy Ghost descended in a bodily shape like a dove upon him, and a voice came from heaven, which said, Thou art my beloved Son; in thee I am well pleased" (Luke 3:21-22).*

The moment the Holy Spirit, in the form of a dove, rested upon Jesus, He was baptized with the Holy Spirit. The dove was an outward manifestation of a spiritual manifestation that took place within Jesus' spirit. As a result of this Baptism of the Holy Spirit, Jesus was filled with the Holy Spirit and immediately was led by the Holy Spirit into the wilderness. But, when He left the wilderness, it was in the "power of the Spirit!" It would appear that the forty days Jesus spent fasting was the final phase of preparation through which He had to pass before entering into His public ministry.

During this 40 days of spiritual preparation, Jesus was "tempted (tried, tested exceedingly) by the devil" (Luke 4:2, AMP). But, Jesus was prepared and met every temptation in total victory. Jesus' physical body may have been tired and weak after not having eaten for forty days. But there was something within Christ that never tired, and is absolutely incapable of being defeated. He was full of the power of the Holy Spirit!

Did He leave this spiritual battleground all beaten, tired and washed out, spiritually drained like so many Christians today after one of Satan's attacks?

No! Jesus returned, *"Full of and under the power of the (Holy) Spirit into Galilee" (Luke 4:14, AMP).* Soon after His forty-day fast, we see Jesus teaching in the synagogue in the power of the Spirit, *"And they were astonished at his doctrine: for his word was with power" (Luke 4:32).* We see Him casting a demon out of a man in the synagogue in the power and authority of the Spirit. When the people saw this "they were all amazed, and spake among themselves, saying, *What a word is this! For with authority and power he commandeth the unclean spirits, and they come out" (Luke 4:36).*

Fasting Will Enable You to Move into a New Dimension of God's Power and Anointing

If the Son of God fasted and prayed before He began His ministry and before He performed any miracles, how much more should we set ourselves apart to fast and pray until we are walking in that same power and anointing of the Holy Spirit, doing the same works Jesus said we would do?

There is a vast difference between being filled with the Spirit and having an experience whereby we are walking in the fullness of the power and authority Christ has made possible. There are many Christians who claim the experience of the Holy Spirit, but when it is time to produce the results, the power and anointing is not there. Many do not really understand what it means for a person to be baptized with the Holy Spirit.

God wants us to move beyond being "filled" with the Spirit into operating in the "power of the Spirit."

There are a lot of Christians who have received an infilling of the Holy Spirit, who have received the gift of the prayer language of the Holy Spirit, and some who have other gifts of the Spirit operating in their lives. But there are very few Christians who have had an experience that is producing the power to bring cripples out of wheelchairs, to open the eyes of the blind, to cause the deaf to hear and the dumb to speak.

God wants us to move beyond being "filled" with the Spirit into operating in the "power of the Spirit." Jesus has promised, *"He that believeth on me, the works that I do shall he do also, and greater works than these shall he do; because I go unto my Father" (John 14:12)* He said, *"It is expedient for you that I go away: for if I go not away, the Comforter will not come unto you; but if I depart, I will send him unto you" (John 16:7).* Jesus made it clear that a result of the Holy Spirit coming upon us will be that we will have the same dunamis miracle working power working in our lives that He had. He said, *"But ye shall receive power, after that the Holy Ghost is come upon you:" (Acts 1:8).*

As you read this book, you may sense a growing hunger to have the fullness of God's power operating in your life. You know that it is possible—Jesus said you would be able to do even greater works. You are hungry—crying out to God for this same type of experience. The Spirit of God is bringing you now to a point in your life where you make a decision and commitment to be willing to do whatever is necessary to come into an even greater relationship with Christ, where the same power and anointing of the Holy Spirit that flowed through Him is flowing through you.

This hungering and thirsting for God to totally possess your being must be the continual desire of your heart. The keys to tapping into the power of the Spirit are prayer and fasting. As you fast and pray, the power of the Spirit will be released in your life as it removes hindrances hindering the flow of the Spirit. When you give yourself to the Lord in a life that is committed to prayer and fasting, His anointing will flow through you in greater and greater power!

Jesus Said, "Man Shall Not Live by Bread Alone, but by Every Word of God"

I want to draw your attention now to the first temptation satan brought before Jesus and Jesus' answer. Look at Luke 4:2, *"Being forty days tempted of the devil. And in those days he did eat nothing: and when they were ended, he afterward hungered."* After not having eaten forty days, Jesus was naturally hungry. And, the first thing satan tempted Him with was food. *"And the devil said unto him, If thou be the Son of God, command this stone that it be made bread" (Luke 4:3).*

Jesus was not taken by surprise. He was prepared. He knew who satan was and why he was there. He knew satan was a deceiver and a liar and had come to tempt Him to sin against God. Jesus used the power of the Word to defeat satan. He responded to this temptation by saying, *"It is written, That man shall not live by bread alone, but by every word of God" (Luke 4:4).*

Jesus had power to turn the stone into bread, but He didn't because it would indicate His failure to trust in His Father's provision. His total dependence was upon His Father and He did nothing separately from Him. Jesus said, *"The Son, can do nothing of himself, but what he seeth the Father do:..." (John 5:19).* His dependence was upon the words that His Father spoke to Him. He said, *"... the words that I speak unto you I speak not of myself: but the Father that dwelleth in me, he doeth the works" (John 14:10), "...the word which ye hear is not mine, but the Father's which sent me" (John 14:24).* This is the same type of total dependence we must have where we have learned that *"man shall not live by bread alone, but by every word of God!"*

> When you fast, you must face the battle of bringing your carnal appetites and fleshly desires into submission of the Spirit.

This Scripture Jesus used in response to this temptation is taken from Deuteronomy 8:3 where Moses reminded the children of Israel why God had allowed them to hunger and fed them with manna forty years during their wanderings in the wilderness. *"And he humbled thee, and suffered thee to hunger, and fed thee with manna, which thou knewest not, neither did thy fathers know; that he might make thee know that man doth not live by bread only, but by every word that proceedeth out of the mouth of the LORD doth man live."*

Fasting Will Enable You to Break the Strongholds of Carnal Appetites and Fleshy Desires

It is interesting to note that one of the first temptations the children of Israel faced after leaving Egypt also involved food. It reveals the extent of the stronghold that had developed in their lives where they were controlled by their carnal appetites and fleshly desires. This example also enables us to see the battle we face when we fast in bringing our carnal appetites and fleshly desires into submission. As you begin your fast, you will see just how strong they are in your life.

It was the fifteenth day of the second month after God supernaturally delivered them out of the cruel Egyptian bondage through mighty signs and wonders. Instead of remembering the awesome miracles He had done on their behalf, the whole congregation began to murmur against Moses and Aaron. They remembered the food they had eaten in Egypt and accused Moses of bringing them out in the wilderness to die from hunger. The people said, *"If only we had died by the LORD's hand in Egypt! There we sat around pots of meat and ate all the food we wanted, but you have brought us out into this desert to starve this entire assembly to death"* *(Exodus 16:3, NIV).*

Fasting breaks strongholds in our lives and enables us to no longer live according to the dictates of our fleshly nature, but by the Holy Spirit.

In other words, their lust and desire for the food they had in Egypt was so strong they would have rather lived under Egyptian bondage and to have died in Egypt than to be free and live under God's leadership and provision in the wilderness.

It is easy to read about this and wonder how that food could have possibly gained such a stronghold in their lives that it would cause them to sin against God. However, as we humble ourselves before God in fasting, God will bring to the surface things in our lives—attitudes, fleshly desires, lusts of our flesh—that need to be brought into submission to the Holy Spirit. There are strong habits; addictions or temptations that we face that can only be overcome as we fast and pray. We must be willing to acknowledge them, repent and crucify them. Paul said, *"But I keep under my body, and bring it into subjection..." (1 Corinthians 10:27).* Through the Holy Spirit we must crucify—put to death our fleshly desires and lusts.

Israel's 40-Year Fast

God said He humbled the children of Israel and allowed them to hunger. In other words, they were put on a type of forced fast where He only allowed them to eat manna for forty years. The reason why God fed them with manna during the 40 years in the wilderness was to teach them to depend upon Him for His daily provision. He was testing them and wanted them to learn to trust Him and live according to all that He spoke to them, not according to their natural desires.

Every morning He rained down food—manna from heaven—to sustain them. They were directed to gather only enough manna for their day's food. The only exception was that on the sixth day they were to gather enough for two days so that they wouldn't have to gather any on the Sabbath. Every day as they went out to gather the manna it was a reminder that God was their Source of provision. Day after day they learned to trust God to provide for their daily sustenance and to live according to His instruction.

This manna provided all the nutrients and ingredients they needed to keep them healthy and strong. There was not one sick person among them during the forty years! However, it wasn't long until the people got tired of eating manna every day. Stop and think about it for a moment. We are often quick to criticize the children of Israel for this. Put yourself in their place. If you had to eat the same thing every day for 40 years, how would you have reacted?

Instead of continuing to depend upon God and His provision, they yielded to their intense craving and lust after the fish, cucumbers, melons, leeks and the other foods they had in Egypt and again began to murmur and complain. "The rabble with them began to crave other food, and again the Israelites started wailing and said, *"If only we had meat to eat! We remember the fish we ate in Egypt at no cost—also the cucumbers, melons, leeks, onions and garlic. But now we have lost our appetite; we never see anything but this manna!"* *(Numbers 11:4-6, NIV).*

The Israelites Yielded to their Lusts and Forfeited God's Blessings

God heard the complaining of the children of Israel and sent them quail in such abundance they stacked it up around their camp two and a half feet deep! God told Moses to tell the people, *"Now the LORD will give you meat, and you will eat it. You will not eat it for just one day, or two days, or five, ten or twenty days, but for a whole month—until it comes out of your nostrils and you loathe it—because you have rejected the Lord, who is among you and have wailed before him, saying, "Why did we ever leave Egypt?" (Numbers 11:18-20, NIV).*

The people ate and ate, and while the meat was still in their mouths God sent a plague and many died. *"But while the meat was still between their teeth and before it could be consumed, the anger of the LORD burned against the people, and he struck them with a severe plague" (Numbers 11:33, NIV).* David recounted their rebellion. He said, *"They soon forgat his works; they waited not for his counsel: But lusted exceedingly in the wilderness, and tempted God in the desert. And he gave them their request; but sent leanness into their soul" (Psalm 106:13-15).*

Instead of continuing to trust in God for His provision, they were controlled by their carnal appetites and lusts of the flesh. As a result, many of them died in the wilderness. God had planned to provide for all their needs and bring them into a land of milk and honey filled with everything they needed. Yet, many of them forfeited God's blessings because they were bound by their carnal appetites and lusts of the flesh.

Fasting Breaks Our Dependence on the Flesh

How does this apply to us today as we consider the importance of fasting?

We, too, must also learn "That man shall not live by bread alone, but by every word of God" (Luke 4:4).

Fasting unto God is a means whereby we bring our natural desires, lusts of the flesh, and appetite under control of the Spirit. It breaks strongholds in our lives and enables us to no longer live according to the dictates of our fleshly nature, but by the Holy Spirit. Instead, we live in trust and dependence upon God and His Word.

There are blessings that God has waiting to release in your life as you are willing to bring your fleshy, carnal desires into submission during seasons of fasting and prayer. Paul said, *"And they that are Christ's have crucified the flesh with the affections and lusts" (Galatians 5:24).* You cannot do this in your own strength, but you must rely on God and His Spirit working in your life.

Fasting is not Optional—It is Expected!

In His teaching on fasting, Jesus made it clear that He expects all those who follow Him as one of His disciples to fast and pray. In His Sermon on the Mount, in Matthew, chapter six He went to the very core of the issue.

In Matthew 6:5-7 Jesus dealt with three major spiritual disciplines expected in the lives of Christians: Giving, prayer and fasting. He dealt first with giving. He didn't say "If you give", He said, *"When you give to the needy, ... "* *(Matthew 6:2, NIV).* Giving is not considered as something optional in our lives. We find that throughout the Word Jesus taught a great deal on the importance of giving, how to give and the rewards of giving.

> Jesus taught fasting as a natural part of the Christian life and explained how we are to fast.

Next, in verses five through seven He taught on prayer. He didn't say, "When you feel like praying…" *No, He said three times, "When you pray…not if.* Beginning with verse seven, we read Jesus' teaching on how we are to pray.

In verses sixteen and seventeen He also didn't say, "If you feel like it or decide some day to fast." He said, *"When you fast..."* Here we see Jesus taught fasting as a natural part of the Christian life and explained how we are to fast.

Jesus Taught Two Major Principles Concerning How to Fast

During Jesus' ministry, fasting had become a legalistic religious practice. The Jews had set aside the second and fifth days of the week as public fast-days. The legalism of the Pharisees had led them to fast on these two days all year long. The rabbinical law stated that on a strict fast a person could not wash or anoint himself and he was not allowed to even greet another person. These two days were also the regular market days when the people came into town from the country. There were special services in the Synagogues, and the local Sanhedrin met, so that these fasting Pharisees would attract and receive special notice for their fastings.

Most of the people who fasted in Jesus' day walked with bowed heads and sad expressions, often putting ashes on their heads and faces in an attempt to appear righteous. In His teaching on fasting, Jesus taught His disciples two important principles on how to fast. He said, *"Moreover when ye fast, be not, as the hypocrites, of a sad countenance: for they disfigure their faces, that they may appear unto men to fast. Verily I say unto you, They have their reward. But thou, when thou fastest, anoint thine head, and wash thy face; That thou appear not unto men to fast, but unto thy Father, which is in secret: and thy Father, which seeth in secret, shall reward thee openly" (Matthew 6:16-18).*

> When you fast, you are to fast unto the Father, neither to be seen by man nor to draw attention to yourself.

Principle #1: Your Fast Must Be Unto God

Jesus dealt first with the wrong motive for fasting. The Pharisee's motive when they fasted was to draw attention to themselves. It was only an outward display. They weren't really fasting unto God, but to be seen by men. He said that they had their reward which was the recognition of men.

When we fast, we are to fast unto the Father, neither to be seen by man nor to draw attention to ourselves. Also, we are not to think that our fasting makes us more righteous or holy than others or that we can earn anything through our good works.

In His parable of the Pharisee and Publican, Jesus made this point clear. The Pharisee prayed with a self-righteous attitude, *"God, I thank thee, that I am not as other men are, extortioners, unjust, adulterers, or even as this publican. I fast twice in the week, I give tithes of all that I possess" (Luke 18:11).* Although the Pharisee prayed, fasted twice a week and gave his tithes, he was not justified before the Father because of his self-righteous attitude.

On the other hand, the publican came humbly before God. He wouldn't even lift up his eyes, but smote his breast and prayed, *"God be merciful to me a sinner" (Luke 18:13).* The publican went to his house justified rather than the Pharisee because of his attitude of humility in approaching God. When we fast, we must approach

God and keep this humble attitude, as I have stressed in previous chapters.

Principle #2: God Rewards Those Who Fast

A second major principle Jesus taught in His discourse in His Sermon on the Mount is that when...not if we fast unto God, He will reward us. We serve a God Who is a Rewarder! *"But without faith it is impossible to please him: for he that cometh to God must believe that he is, and that he is a rewarder of them that diligently seek him" (Hebrews 11:6).* God rewards those who fast! Jesus said, *"...thy Father, which seeth in secret, shall reward thee openly" (Matthew 6:18).* Jesus linked fasting with benefits that would have outward tangible, visible results.

All the fasts recorded in the Bible—whether one day, three days, twenty-one days or forty days brought visible rewards:

- Joshua and the elders of Israel kept a solemn fast when they were defeated by the armies of Ai. They remained prostrate on their faces before the Ark, with dust on their heads in deep humiliation and prayer. *"And Joshua rent his clothes, and fell to the earth upon his face before the ark of the LORD until the eventide, he and the elders of Israel, and put dust upon their heads" (Joshua 7:6).*

God rewarded their fasting after Joshua dealt with the sin that was exposed in the camp. God delivered their enemies into their hands and they defeated the armies of Ai. (See Joshua 8:1, 24-29)

• David fasted and prayed seven days as he humbled himself under the judgment of God sent upon him for his sin of adultery with Bathseba and in killing her husband Uriah. *"David therefore besought God for the child; and David fasted, and went in, and lay all night upon the earth" (2 Samuel 12:16).* As long as the child was alive David fasted and wept. But, on the seventh day his son died. After he died, David arose from the earth, washed, anointed himself, changed clothes, went to the house of the Lord and worshipped.

David's reward: Although his son died, God saw David's heart, forgave him and gave him another son, Solomon, who would one day reign as king.

- When Nehemiah was still in Babylon, he heard about the desolations of Jerusalem and the people of God and set apart a season of prayer and fasting. *"And it came to pass, when I heard these words, that I sat down and wept, and mourned certain days, and fasted, and prayed before the God of heaven"* (Nehemiah 1:4). Nehemiah's reward: *God gave Nehemiah favor with King Artaxerxes who sent captains of his army and horsemen to accompany Nehemiah on his journey to Jerusalem and gave him the wood from his forests to build the walls and gates of Jerusalem. (Nehemiah 2:8-9).*

- When Jonah proclaimed God's impending judgments upon Ninevah, the people immediately set apart a season of prayer and fasting. *"So the people of Nineveh believed God, and proclaimed a fast, and put on sackcloth, from the greatest of them even to the least of them"* (Jonah 3:5). When the word reached the king of Ninevah, he took off his royal robes and covered himself with sackcloth and sat in ashes. Then he sent out a proclamation calling everyone in Ninevah to fast, including the animals. He said, *"Let neither man nor beast, herd nor flock, taste any thing: let them not feed, nor drink water; But let man and beast be covered with sackcloth, and cry mightily unto God; yea, let them turn every one from his evil way, and from the violence that is in their hand.*

God's reward: Although Ninevah was exceedingly sinful, God rewarded their fast by sparing the city. *"And God saw their works, that they turned from their evil way; and God repented of the evil, that he said that he would do unto them; and he did it not" (Jonah 3:10).*

• When Queen Esther and the Jews faced destruction at the hand of Haman, she called a three day fast. She told Mordecai, *"Go, gather together all the Jews that are present in Shushan, and fast ye for me, and neither eat nor drink three days, night or day: I also and my maidens will fast likewise…" (Esther 4:14).*

God's reward: He turned the circumstances around on behalf of Esther, Mordecai and the Jews. The king issued decrees reversing Haman's orders to destroy the Jews throughout all the provinces, Haman was hanged and the King granted the Jews in every city to defend themselves and to take the spoils. (Esther 8:7-11)

When You Fast—Expect God To Reward You

When you fast and pray with the right motives and according to the way God has revealed through His Word, expect Him to reward you openly. Expect miracles to follow! In addition to the ten major benefits of fasting mentioned in chapter four, there are many more benefits too innumerable to mention. Here are just a few additional benefits you can expect when you fast:

- A greater level of intimacy with the Father.

- Increased sensitivity to the Holy Spirit.

- Personal and corporate revival.

- Increased anointing.

- Financial breakthroughs.

- Physical breakthroughs.

- Deliverance from evil habits and lusts of the flesh.

- Demonic strongholds destroyed.

It is important to remember that while we know that God does reward fasting, the rewards He gives are not earned or deserved by us because of our fasting. We can never earn God's favor or rewards, but can only receive them. As we fast, we humble ourselves before God which positions us to receive from Him.

God Rewards Man on 40-Day Fast With Supernatural Healing of Cancer

In his book, *The 21 Day Fast,* Dr. Bob Rodgers, Senior Pastor of Evangel World Prayer Center in Louisville, Kentucky, shares the following testimony illustrating God's power that was released in the life of a friend who went on a 40-Day fast. Pastor Rodgers is used mightily in the area of prayer and fasting and leads his congregation on a yearly 21 Day fast at the beginning of the year.

> When you fast and pray with the right motives and according to the way God has revealed through His Word, expect God's reward!

A friend of mine developed a growth on his ear. He went to this doctor in his church. The doctor said, "Pastor,

I want you to see a specialist, that could be cancer." So he went to the specialist. It was diagnosed as fast spreading melanoma. The doctor urged, "If we do not operate immediately and take some of this ear off, you could die." He told the doctor, "Well, before I do that, I feel like I should fast and pray." He went on a 40-day fast.

While he was on the fast, he was asked to come and pray for a woman who was bedridden. He went into the room where her husband was kneeling on the other side of the bed. She was lying there, bound by demons. From her position, she couldn't see this growth on his ear. Without even looking at him, these demons spoke out of her and said, "Hugh". She laughed a blood-curdling laugh. The demons said, "Do you expect to get demons out of me, when you cannot even get yourself healed of cancer of the ear." She laughed again.

It made him so angry, he turned and walked out of the room, and walked into the bathroom of this house. He said, "You foul devil, you will not destroy me with cancer." He reached up and grabbed the melanoma on his ear and jerked it right off his ear. The blood began to go everywhere. He washed himself and got a towel.

It finally stopped bleeding. He walked back and cast the demons out of that woman and she was totally healed.

He went back home. The next Sunday he was in church, and this same doctor came up and said, "Oh pastor, let me see that ear. That operation that the doctor did was a good operation. That thing looks like you never had cancer before." [1]

God Rewards Prayer and Fasting With an Awesome Demonstration of His Mighty Healing Power!

As noted in chapter two, Jesus taught the power that is released through prayer and fasting when He said, *"If ye have faith as a grain of a mustard seed, ye shall say unto this mountain, remove hence to yonder place; and it shall remove: and nothing shall be impossible to you. Howbeit, this kind goeth not out but by prayer and fasting"* (Matthew 17:20-21).

Throughout my ministry, I have dedicated myself to fasting and prayer and have often spent days and weeks fasting in preparation for upcoming ministry outreaches. As a result, I have seen God's supernatural power manifested through tremendous miracles of healing and deliverance.

One of the most outstanding miracles that I will never forget was in the life of a crippled man whose body was terribly twisted. His situation was totally hopeless—beyond any natural cure, until Jesus met Him, healed his body and set him free!

> When prevailing in prayer for needs that are very urgent or resistant, fasting is often used by the Holy Spirit to give extra power; to bring Satan's defeat and Christ's victory into view.
>
> Wesley L. Duewel

I was in the Dominican Republic conducting an evangelistic crusade. Great crowds were coming to the meetings every night. People were getting saved and there were many miracles of healing.

A large group had organized a big rally to come against our meetings. One night they began to throw rocks at me as I preached. I remember that night as if it were only yesterday. One of the rocks that had been thrown toward me on the stage fell to the floor before it reached me as if there had been some type of physical shield around me.

No one in the crowd was injured except for a lady who received a little cut from one of the rocks.

The next night, the crowd was double what it was the previous night. There were about 20,000 there. There were a lot of visitors and pastors in the meeting from different parts of the United States.

After I had preached and ministered for an extensive period of time, I was tired and worn out—soaking wet with sweat.

Before Me Was a Crippled Man Whose Body Was Terribly Twisted

Just as I was ready to close the service and leave the platform, my interpreter, the Overseer of the Church of God in Puerto Rico, told me, "Brother Lowery, can you pray for one more person?" He said, "We have a man who is crippled and we want you to pray for him."

I didn't know how crippled he was. At that moment some men were laying a man on the platform whose legs were drawn and twisted up under him. His arms were also twisted and drawn. He could not walk nor use his arms.

Everyone in town knew who he was. He was the man that people moved from one street corner to another so that he could beg.

I walked over to where he was laying.

As I reached out to lay my hands on him and pray, the Lord pulled my hands back.

"I'm going to heal the man tonight, but don't lay your hands upon him. I must have all the honor and glory," the Lord told me.

I waited for a moment. By this time all the ministers from the United States and the missionaries had gathered around where I was standing.

Then I began to pray, *"Silver and gold have I none..."*. Simultaneously as I prayed, all the other ministers and missionaries began to pray it with me: *"Silver and gold have I none; but such as I have give I thee: In the name of Jesus Christ of Nazareth rise up and walk (Acts 3:6).*

The Man's Bones Began To Crack and Pop!

While we were praying, I heard the bones begin to crack and pop in his hands.

The man began to shake and tremble under the power of Almighty God.

His hands straightened out!

By this time, my hair was standing up on my head and down the back of my neck.

He started crying and said, "It feels like there are some nails sticking in my legs. The blood started circulating in his legs and they began to do the same thing. He was shaking and the bones in his legs were cracking and popping.

I took the man by his hand and lifted him to his feet.

This hopeless paralytic, who had been bound and twisted all his life stood to his feet. He was as tall as I am. He started walking back and forth across the platform and pandemonium broke out!

Upon seeing this awesome miracle manifested in the life of the paralytic man, seven to eight thousand people came rushing up to the front crying and wanting to be saved.

The man, once twisted and paralyzed, jumped off the platform and climbed over a cement wall about four feet high. I can see it now! He started walking down the road and a man on crutches came out from the side of the road. The man on crutches placed his hand on the paralytic man who had been healed. He dropped his crutches— instantly healed by the power of God! He knew that if he just touched that man who had received such an incredible miracle that he would be healed. And he was!

When you fast and pray according to God's Word, expect God to reward you openly. Remember, Jesus said, *"...thy Father, which seeth in secret, shall reward thee openly" (Matthew 6:18).* Don't limit God! Expect Him to release the things into your life that you need. Expect breakthroughs in every area of your life! Expect God to release His miracle power to flow through you in a greater measure.

Prayer + Fasting + Giving Positions You to Receive God's Blessings and Provision!

In the Word we read about Cornelius, a Gentile centurion, *"A devout man, and one that feared God with all his house, which gave much alms to the people, and prayed to God always" (Acts 10:2)*. One day as Cornelius was fasting and praying, an angel appeared to him. Cornelius gives us this account, *"Four days ago I was fasting until this hour: and at the ninth hour I prayed in my house, and behold, a man stood before me in bright clothing. And said, Cornelius, thy prayer is heard, and thine alms are had in remembrance in the sight of God" (Acts 10:30-31)*.

Here, in the life of Cornelius, we see three key elements that resulted in a tremendous breakthrough with the Holy Spirit being poured out upon his entire household: Prayer, fasting and giving. Cornelius was fasting, praying and diligently seeking God when God sent an angel to him. In chapter ten, verse four we read that the angel told Cornelius, *"Thy prayers and thine alms are come up for a memorial before God" (Acts 10:4)*. His fasting, prayers and gifts to the poor ascended up before God as a sweet-smelling savour. It became a living memorial before God and God openly rewarded Cornelius.

Cornelius' prayers were answered and the door for the Gentiles was opened with a great outpouring of the Spirit. While Peter was still ministering, the Holy Spirit was poured out upon Cornelius' household and all those who had come together in Cornelius' house. The Jews who had accompanied Peter were amazed, *"For they heard them speak with tongues, and magnify God" (Acts 10:46).*

Fasting + Prayer + Giving touches God's heart

Fasting + Prayer + Giving touches God's heart. It is a living memorial before God and He will reward you!

Fasting Breaks Poverty

Are you ready for your financial breakthrough?

In his book, *21-Day Fast*, Pastor Bob Rodgers shares the following from his wealth of experience concerning how fasting has brought financial breakthrough to many people who have participated in his yearly 21-day fast.

Fasting breaks the power of poverty. To some this

may come as a shock, but It is really true. I discovered that as I plant a seed each time I fast, a major blessing returns to me quickly.

Over the years I have seen many hundreds of people with low-paying jobs, people who couldn't afford a home or good automobile, and businesses facing financial troubles. God turned it around as they fasted and prayed. During the spring and summer, scores of couples in our church will be moving into new homes. It happens every year.

> Fasting + Prayer + Giving will break poverty off your life and positions you to receive God's financial provision and blessing.

If you will have a lifestyle of fasting, you will begin to see prosperity come to you. This is not saying that if you fast one time you are going to be rich. But, if you fast continually, God will bless you financially in a way you have never dreamed.[2]

One of the seven prophetic promises I mentioned in chapter one, that God said He would do as the children of Israel responded to the call of fasting and prayer was to break their poverty and release His blessings. Look at these promises in Joel once again. God said, *"Behold I will send you corn, and wine, and oil and you shall be satisfied therewith...* *(Joel 2:19)* He said, *"And the floors shall be full of wheat, and the vats shall overflow with wine and oil"* *(Joel 2:24), "And you shall eat in plenty, and be satisfied..." (Joel 2:26).*

Fasting + Prayer + Giving will break poverty off your life and positions you to receive God's financial provision and blessing. You may be facing severe financial problems, overdue bills, insufficient income to cover your monthly expenses or possibly foreclosure on your house. When you fast, humble yourself before God. Seek His face. Get into the Word of God and let it go deep into your Spirit. Spend time in prayer, not just asking God for His hand of favor and blessing, but worshipping and praising Him for Who He is.

Then, add giving to your fasting and prayer. Give a special offering, help someone else in need, give to the poor and release your faith expecting God's provision and blessing to be released in your circumstances. Before you see any outward manifestation or change in your circumstances begin to praise and thank God for meeting your needs. Jesus said, *"What things soever ye desire, when ye pray, believe that ye receive them, and ye shall have them" (Mark 11:24).*

In his book, *Fasting,* Jentezen Franklin shared the following story of a woman who received a tremendous financial breakthrough as she joined with his church in their yearly 21-day fast:

Susan had worked at one company for fifteen years but lost her job when they were bought out by another company. Making matters more overwhelming, in December, Susan's thirty-five-year-old brother died suddenly, leaving her deeply grieved and brokenhearted. She found the grace to join the fast with the church at the beginning of the year. To her amazement, the company contacted her in March and said, "We're going to give you a year's salary and extended benefits for a full year." With that money, she and her husband became debt free, except for their home, and were able to purchase a newer vehicle. She later told us that, as a result of the fast, God had restored her desire to live.[3]

Christ Intends Fasting to be an Integral Part of Your Life

Within the Church there are many who ask themselves, "Why is fasting so important?" and "Why should I fast?" Although there are not any rigid rules given in the Word concerning fasting, from Christ's teaching on fasting we clearly see that it is not a matter of "if"— whether or not Christians should fast—but "when!". Fasting should be an integral part and discipline of every follower of Christ.

When the disciples of John the Baptist came to Jesus asking Him why His disciples didn't fast, Jesus made it clear that a time would come when His disciples would fast. John the Baptist lived a fasted lifestyle and his disciples fasted often in compliance with John's example, for John *"came neither eating nor drinking..." (Matthew 11:18).* In addition to his other times of fasting, John no doubt observed the same Jewish fast days observed by the Pharisees.

John's disciples asked Jesus, *"How is it that we and the Pharisees fast, but your disciples do not fast?" (Matthew 9:14, NIV)* As already noted, by the time of the

New Testament, Judaism regarded fasting as a meritorious work. When Jesus fasted, He did not regard it as earning favor with God nor was it simply a religious practice to be observed. He had inaugurated His earthly ministry by fasting forty days, taught and demonstrated the power of fasting.

He answered their question with a question. He asked them, *"How can the guests of the bridegroom mourn while he is with them? The time will come when the bridegroom will be taken from them; then they will fast" (Matthew 9:15, NIV).* Jesus used the analogy of the bridegroom and wedding feast to give an answer to John's disciples. According to Rabbinic law, the wedding feast was to be a time of great festivity. Even on the holiest day of the Mosaic Law, the Day of Atonement, when fasting was specifically commanded by the Law, the bride and bridegroom were allowed to forego that requirement. All mourning was to be suspended during the marriage week.

Jesus Revealed a Time was Coming When His Disciples Would Fast

The answer that Jesus gave in this verse is very significant and relevant to the Church of Jesus Christ today. In these verses Jesus was referring to Himself as the Bridegroom. You will note that in the King James Version, verse nine translates "the guests of the bridegroom" as the "children of the bridegroom." Both these terms refer to the disciples. Jesus was saying that while He was with the disciples, it was not the time for fasting.

Fasting was associated with a time of mourning, sorrow, and weeping. While Jesus was with them, it was not a time for mourning but a time for joy. The kingdom of God had come, and as long as He was with them, it was a time of rejoicing. Demons fled. Sickness vanished. The lame walked and the blind saw. There was no sorrow whatsoever associated with Jesus.

However, Jesus spoke of a time that would come when He (the Bridegroom) would be taken, and then would come a time for fasting and weeping. He knew that He would be crucified, resurrected in great power and return to the Father, leaving His disciples to carry on the work He had given them to do. He knew they would face intense persecution and death and there would be a great need to fast and pray in order to walk in power and victory over all the satanic forces that would be unleashed against them.

Now is the Time to Fast and Pray!

Friend, now is the appointed time for the Church… the Bride of Christ…to fast!

Our heavenly Bridegroom has been taken from us. Jesus has ascended into heaven and now the time has come when we need to walk in the power and anointing of God that is released through prayer and fasting.

We are living in a time of great turmoil and perplexity. Governments are crumbling. Natural disasters, floods, earthquakes, famine and drought plague the nations. We live with the threat of terrorist attacks, chemical warfare and the possibility of a nuclear war and are struggling to find solutions to the problems we face with the global recession.

If ever there was a time when the Bride of Christ needs to hear the call of the Bridegroom to fast—it is now!

God is raising up a prayer army of invincible, spiritual warriors in every nation who, like Ezra, Nehemiah and Daniel, will set their faces to fast and pray, weep and mourn on behalf of the sins of the people in their surrounding communities, cities and nations. He will use these men and women to lead the Church in true repentance. And through their prayer and fasting, they will bring down God's power and release salvation, healing, and deliverance upon their cities and nations.

You can be one of them…if you will hear the call of the Spirit, consecrate yourself and make fasting part of your lifestyle.

The only way you will be able to break through barriers and tear down strongholds in your life, family, city and nation is to get on your face before God in times of prayer and fasting and stay there until you know that satan's power has been broken.

Now is the appointed time for the Church... the Bride of Christ... to fast!

The great spiritual warrior Daniel stayed before the Lord in prayer and fasting 21 days before He received the answer He was seeking. While he was fighting this great battle in prayer and fasting, there was an intense spiritual battle going on in the heavenlies where demonic forces had built a line of resistance to hinder Daniel from receiving the answer he needed. In chapter six we will look more closely at fasting as a powerful spiritual weapon to break demonic strongholds and how it is a powerful weapon that positions you to be heard and to prevail with God.

FASTING
THAT MOVES
GOD'S HAND

Chapter Six

Can We ... Will We?

"If ye have faith as a grain of mustard seed, ye shall say
unto this mountain, Remove hence to yonder place; and
it shall remove; and nothing shall be impossible unto you.
Howbeit this kind goeth not out but by prayer and fasting. "
Matthew 17:20-21

chapter six

Can We ... Will We?

Through prayer and fasting you can move God's hand!

I am not talking about fasting in an attempt to impress God or manipulate Him to do your bidding. But rather humbling yourself through fasting which positions you to hear and receive from God!

> God has given the Church the awesome responsibility and privilege through prayer and fasting to move His hand on behalf of our families, cities and nations. It is not a matter of can we do it, but will we?

As you have seen in the examples mentioned throughout this book, whenever we humble ourselves through fasting and prayer, according to the principles established in His Word, God responds. He supernaturally intervenes in our circumstances, stretches His mighty hand toward us and meets our needs!

- When Moses fasted forty days in intercession on behalf of the children of Israel, he moved God's hand to spare their lives. *"And the LORD repented of the evil which he thought to do unto his people"* *(Exodus 32:14).*

- Through prayer and fasting the wicked King Ahab moved God's hand to withhold His judgment that had been pronounced upon him and his descendents because of his wickedness. God told Elijah, *"...because he humbleth himself before me, I will not bring the evil in his days: but in his son's days will I bring the evil upon his house"* *(1 Kings 21:29).*

- As Samuel and the children of Israel fasted, they moved God's hand. Not only did He fight for them until their enemies were defeated before them, *"the hand of the LORD was against the Philistines all the days of Samuel"* *(1 Samuel 7:13)* God restored all the cities which the Philistines had taken from Israel and there was peace.

- When the king of Ninevah and the people fasted, they moved God's hand to withhold His judgment and their city was spared. *"And God saw their works, that they turned from their evil way; and God repented of the evil, that he said that he would do unto them; and he did it not" (Jonah 3:10).*

• As the early Church fasted and prayed, they moved God's hand on behalf of Peter who was facing certain death at the hands of Herod. God dispatched an angel who broke his chains off and delivered him out of prison. (Acts 12:1-17).

Fasting touches God's heart and brings heavenly rewards. In chapter four we looked at Christ's teaching on fasting in His Sermon on the Mount where He said our fasting is to be *"unto thy Father which is in secret: and thy Father, which seeth in secret, shall reward thee openly" (Matthew 6:18).*

> When you fast, have the same strong determination as Daniel to seek God diligently until you receive the answer you need.

When you fast, set your spiritual focus on what you need expecting to move God's hand and reward you with an answer.

When You Fast, Be Led By The Spirit

As you respond to God's call to fast, remember there are no set rules and regulations so do not fall into the trap of becoming legalistic about it. The most important thing is to be led by the Spirit regarding the type and length of your fast. You may feel led to fast one meal a day for a determined amount of time, fast one or two days a week, or go on a fast, drinking water only, for 1 day, 3 days, 7 days, 21 days or longer.

The saints in the Old and New Testaments fasted and sought God until they obtained what they desired. When Daniel understood by studying the word of the Lord through Jeremiah that the determined amount of years when Israel's desolation would be over and God would deliver the children of Israel out of captivity, he said, *"I set my face unto the Lord God, to seek by prayer and supplications, with fasting, and sackcloth and ashes" (Daniel 9:3).* Daniel "set" his face to seek the Lord. He was determined to stay on his face

> Fasting strengthens your prayer priorities, focuses your prevailing, and enables you to give uninterrupted concentration to prevailing intercession.
> Wesley L. Duewel

230

before God in fasting and prayer until He obtained what He needed from God.

When you begin your fast, make the same determination as Daniel to seek God diligently until you receive the answer you need. Refuse to become intimidated by the devil who will tempt you to break your fast prematurely. He doesn't want you to fast because he knows the power that is released through consecrated fasting and prayer. Well intentioned family members and friends may also try to convince you to compromise or break your fast due to their concern for your health. Stay focused on God, the purpose of your fast and upon God's promises.

The Absolute or Complete Fast

There are basically three types of fasts recorded in the Word:

1. The absolute or complete fast.

2. The normal fast.

3. The partial fast.

The absolute or complete fast refers to a total fast in which a person eats or drinks nothing. The maximum time for this type of fast is three days and nights. If a person goes any longer than three days without water (except in the literal presence of God as in Moses' fast), he faces serious health risks. One of the greatest examples of the complete fast is the fast Queen Esther called and observed along with Mordecai and the Jews throughout Shushan. Esther told Mordecai to gather all the Jews throughout Shushan and call them to fast. She said, *"...and fast ye for me, and neither eat nor drink three days, night or day: I also and my maidens will fast likewise..." (Esther 4:15)*. Realizing this was a life and death situation, Esther called all the Jews throughout Shushan to participate.

The Normal Fast

The normal fast involves abstention from food drinking water only. This is the type of fast Jesus observed in the wilderness. Jesus was led by the Spirit into the wilderness, *"Being forty days tempted of the devil. And in those days he did eat nothing: and when they were ended, he afterward hungered" (Luke 4:2)*. It is clear in the Scriptures that during Jesus' forty day fast he didn't eat anything and when his fast ended he was hungry. However, there is no mention of Jesus not drinking during His fast nor that when His fast was over He was thirsty. He most likely drank a lot of water.

When you observe this type of fast, it is best if you drink plenty of water. This is one of the best ways to flush all the poisons out of your system. Some people squeeze a little lemon juice into the water to increase the cleansing effect. There are also those who observe this type of fast who drink clear broth and juices at times to maintain their strength.

The Partial Fast

The partial fast is often referred to as the "Daniel fast" and is based upon Daniel's fast referred to in Daniel 10:1-3. Daniel said, *"I ate no pleasant bread; neither came flesh nor wine in my mouth, neither did I anoint myself at all, till three whole weeks were fulfilled" (Daniel 10:3).* The "pleasant bread" mentioned in this verse translated from the original Hebrew means "bread of desires."

It refers to bread made of the finest wheat that was eaten in the courts of the princes where Daniel was. In general it means the best of bread.

During his 21-day fast, as Daniel humbled himself before God, he chose not to eat of the "bread of desires" the choice foods that were prepared for him in the courts of the princes. He not only didn't eat the "pleasant bread" he also did not eat any of the choice meats or drink any wine. There is actually no indication that he ate any type of food during his fast.

People who observe the Daniel fast eat no desserts or meat and eat only vegetables and fruits. As I stated in chapter three, I do not discount this type of partial fast. There are many people today with certain types of physical conditions or limitations who are physically unable to go on a water only fast and choose to go on the Daniel fast. However, if you have no physical conditions preventing you, I recommend that you observe the normal fast eating no food but drinking water.

Regardless of whether you observe a complete, normal or partial fast, if you are truly fasting unto God, you can expect His hand to be moved on your behalf and those for whom you are praying. Expect God's divine intervention in your circumstances! The length or type of fast isn't the most important thing. The most important consideration is that you fast with the right motives as emphasized throughout this book.

Understanding The Physical Benefits of Fasting

In addition to the tremendous spiritual benefits of fasting I have shared with you, there are also some physical benefits you need to know about as well. As you begin your fast, you need to be aware of the physical changes and challenges you will face and the resulting benefits.

- During an extended fast of three days or more, your body will go through physical adjustments. Be aware that the first three or four days will be the most difficult as hunger pangs and physical discomforts may intensify before subsiding around the fourth day.

- Fasting helps flush poisons and toxins out of

your system. You will notice a sort of coating on your tongue for a few days. It is a sign the fast is helping your body eliminate toxins. Bottled water should be taken in large quantities before and during the fast.

• As a person fasts, his pores become laden with toxins, especially his hands and face. Much more waste is removed through our pores during a fast, than at any other time. A person should bathe as often as possible. In about two weeks the average individual will have most of the wastes, poisons and toxins eliminated.

• Fasting gives your digestive system a rest. During the first three days of a fast, most people feel sluggish and experience headaches which are the result of the impurities and poisons the body is burning. After three days, the headaches usually disappear. Keep drinking plenty of water and those toxins which poison your body will be flushed out.

• Toxins are also flushed out of the kidneys through the urine. The urine turns darker indicating that the disease-causing poison and toxins are being washed out. Drink at least six glasses of bottled water daily.

• The same amount of poison is released through the nostrils and lungs, as through the kidneys, bowels and skin. Bad breath is also an indication that the body is being cleansed of toxins. The vapor that comes from the lungs will clear up and the breath will become clean and odorless as that of a baby.

• After several days of the fast have passed, the hunger appetite leaves. If the fast is prolonged; in a week, ten days or more, the weakness leaves and the average person feels even stronger than he did before he began to fast.

• There are many medical benefits of fasting. In his book, *101 Reasons to Fast*, Pastor Bob Rodgers cites medical reports indicating that fasting is a means of healing the body. He refers to Dr. Oda H. F. Birchinger, who has supervised more than 70,000 fasts, and who states, "Fasting can heal and help rheumatism in the joints and muscles, diseases of the heart, circulation, blood vessels, stress-related exhaustion, skin diseases— including pimples and complexion problems, irregular menstrual cycles and hot flashes, disease of respiratory organs, allergies such as hay fever and other eye diseases."[1]

• Fasting lowers your blood pressure and can lower your cholesterol.

• It has been proven that fasting sharpens your mental process and aids and improves your sight, hearing, taste, touch, smell and all sensory faculties.

• Fasting breaks the addiction to junk food.

Fasting Guidelines

Here are a few practical guidelines that will be helpful to you as you fast and develop fasting as a lifestyle:

1. After determining the type and length of your fast, determine the major purpose for your fast: Are you fasting for:

- A personal breakthrough in your life—spiritually, physically or mentally.

- Healing in your body or in the life of a loved one.

- A financial breakthrough.

- Salvation of family members and loved ones.

- Restoration in your marriage and family relationships.

- For a greater manifestation of God's power and anointing in your life.

- Guidance in making important decisions.

- God's divine intervention in crisis situations in other nations.

- Personal and corporate revival.

- Spiritual breakthroughs in your community and city with bondages being broken and people being set free from drugs, alcohol, prostitution, and souls being won into the kingdom of God.

2. Set your spiritual focus. As much as possible, shut out worldly distractions. If you are working during your fast, set aside your lunch hour and find a quiet place where you can be alone to read your Bible, pray and commune with God every day. At home turn off the television and spend the time you normally would

When you fast, set your spiritual focus and dedicate as much time as possible to reading the Word and listening to hear Him speak to you.

239

be eating your meal in prayer and worshipping God. Find a quiet place where you can be alone with God, preferably where you can play worship music and create an atmosphere where God can speak to you. Dedicate as much time as possible to reading and studying the Word, waiting on the Lord and listening to hear Him speak to you. During the fast you may become weak and not feel like praying. If this happens, don't become discouraged but keep in mind that the fasting process is a constant prayer unto God.

3. Write down your greatest needs and pray specifically over each need during your time of fasting. Set your faith and don't waiver in what you are asking of God.

4. Several days leading up to your fast, start eating smaller portions of food. Stop drinking liquids containing caffeine and cut down on desserts and foods containing a high concentration of sugar.

5. On the first day of your fast try to drink as much purified or distilled water as possible and continue to drink plenty of water throughout your fast.

6. If you have a medical condition such as diabetes,

heart disease or a chronic health problem, be sure to consult a doctor before starting your fast. You may want to make a commitment to limiting your food intake to one salad on the day you fast or to eating only vegetables.

7. If you drink fruit juices, avoid the acidic juices like orange and grapefruit juices.

8. It is very important that you break your fast properly to avoid injuring your stomach. Start by drinking diluted juices, eating things like oatmeal, chicken broth and soups. Take as much time to break your fast, especially in adding meat back into your diet, as the length of your fast.

9. During your time of fasting, your bowels have been dormant. To regain your regularity, eat soft foods with fiber. If the fast is seven days or less, it can be broken by eating whole fresh fruit for two or three meals on the first day; light soups on the second day; green vegetables on the third day and your regular diet from that point forward. Even after a short fast of two or three days, break your fast gradually eating soups and light meals.

God's Purposes for This End-Time Universal Call to Prayer and Fasting

Now that you have considered the physical benefits of fasting and have practical guidelines concerning how to fast, let us look more closely at God's purposes for this end time mobilization of the Church for united fasting and prayer.

As we have seen in the examples of fasting saints in the Old and New Testaments, there were corporate and individual fasts, different types of fasts as well as many varied reasons why they fasted. In addition to these, I want you to consider the following major reasons why I believe God is issuing this end-time universal call to prayer and fasting to the Church.

> First and foremost, I believe this end time call to fasting and prayer is a call to the Church for repentance!

1. To humble ourselves before Him in repentance and receive His grace, forgiveness and mercy.

First and foremost, I believe this is a call to repentance within the Church. As I emphasized in chapter one, not only do we need to set ourselves apart in seasons of personal fasting and prayer where we are confessing and repenting of sin in our lives, the Church needs to unite in seasons of corporate fasting to repent for the sins that have crept into the Church. Before we can be used by God in the fullness of His power to help bring salvation, healing and transformation to our cities and nations, we must allow the Holy Spirit to do a deep work of cleansing and bring true holiness back into the Church.

2. To believe Him for an end-time outpouring of His Spirit and a sweeping worldwide revival.

In his book, *The Hidden Power of Prayer and Fasting,* Mahesh Chavda emphasizes God's call to corporate fasting. He states:

The Lord's word on corporate prayer has nothing to do with following programs, agendas, or the thinking of people. It has everything to do with being involved in

Spirit-led submitted prayer. Our task is simply to come together and harmonize in prayer and worship in God's presence, offering ourselves to Him in love and adoration; while making ourselves available to stand in the gap for others, to obey His every instruction, and then to simply wait until He shows up.[2]

Within the Church we must be willing to lay aside our denominational differences and religious traditions and unite in one mind and one accord as the 120 did in the upper room. "And when the day of Pentecost was fully come, they were all with one accord in one place" (Acts 2:1).

Never underestimate the power of unity in prayer! As the 120 united in prayer—in expectation—of the promised baptism of the Holy Spirit, they moved the hand of God! A supernatural, heavenly sound, "as of a rushing mighty wind" filled the place. The 120 were filled with the Holy Ghost and began to speak in other tongues, giving testimony of the wonderful works of God. (Acts 4-11). The disciples began doing the works of God in a mighty demonstration of the power and anointing Christ had promised until they reached the entire known world with the Gospel! They walked in the supernatural power of Almighty God! *"...and many wonders and signs were done by the apostles"* (Acts 2:43). They healed the sick, cast out devils and raised the dead!

As we fast and pray, we must cry out:

"Lord, do it again! We need Your power flowing through us to reach our cities and nations in the same mighty demonstration of power that You said we would. Lord, do it again! Baptize us with the power of Your Spirit enabling us to heal the sick, cast out devils and raise the dead. Change us! Remove every obstacle in our lives that hinders the flow of Your Spirit. Set us on fire with Your Spirit and use us to reach and win the lost, those who are hurting, bound by sin—without hope. Lord, do it again!"

> As we unite in seasons of fasting and prayer, we must cry out, "Lord, do it again!"

3. To come before Him in repentance and intercession on behalf of our nations and believe Him for city-wide and nation-wide transformation.

God's promise to the Church is, *"Ask of me, and I shall give thee the heathen for thine inheritance, and the uttermost parts of the earth for thy possession" (Psalm 2:8).* We must be like Moses, Ezra and Daniel who fasted and interceded on behalf of the children of Israel.

• Moses was in such anguish on behalf of the sins of the people, he cried out to God, *"Yet now, if thou wilt forgive their sin--; and if not, blot me, I pray thee, out of thy book which thou hast written" (Exodus 32:32).*

• Ezra was so distressed by the sins the people had committed he tore his garment, plucked out hair off his head and beard *"and set down astonied" (Ezra 9:3).*

• Daniel cried out for God's mercy, *"O Lord, hear; O lord, forgive; O Lord, hearken and do; defer not, for thine own sake, O my God: for thy city and thy people are called by thy name" (Daniel 9:19).*

In chapter four we looked at Isaiah 58 and considered the fast that is acceptable to God. He doesn't want us to just go through the outward motions of fasting and prayer.

In addition to the time we set apart for prayer and fasting, God expects us to break the yokes of bondage off those in our neighborhoods, communities, at the marketplace and everywhere we go. Prayer + Fasting + Action is what God is calling for when we fast.

We must loose the bands of wickedness!

We must undo the heavy burdens!

We must set the captives free!

We must break every yoke!

4. To bring us into a greater revelation of Himself and a new dimension of intimacy.

This is perhaps the most important reason why God is releasing this universal end-time call of fasting and prayer. He is calling us to shut out the world with all its distractions and to spend time alone with Him. He wants us to seek His face and not just His hand of blessing. When God directed David to seek His face, David responded, *"...my heart said unto thee, Thy face LORD, will I seek" (Psalm 27:8).*

This is the attitude we need as we respond to His call. We need to be so hungry for Him that everything within us is crying out:

"Father, I need You more than life itself. I long for You. I want to know You in Your fullness. Show me Your glory! Draw me close to You and reveal what is on Your heart. Speak to me and open my understanding with a greater revelation of You."

With all my heart I believe that we need a greater revelation of the holiness, power and glory of God Almighty. We need to wait in His presence like Moses did in fasting and prayer until God's glory saturates our beings. We need to know Him intimately so that we will clearly hear His voice and know what He is saying in this end-time hour.

Your greatest desire during your fast must be seeking to know God in a greater level of intimacy. David was a man after God's own heart who lived in intimate communion and fellowship with Him. He said, *"One thing have I desired of the LORD, that will I seek after: that I may dwell in the house of the LORD all the days of my life, to behold the beauty of the LORD, and to enquire in his temple" (Psalm 27:4).* David passionately pursued God. He focused His entire being on seeking after God and made it his top priority. When you fast, make it your number one priority and set your spiritual focus on seeking after God.

Pastors, evangelists and ministers, hours of preparation and Bible study cannot compare to the revelation and anointing you will receive shut away in His Presence, waiting upon Him, allowing Him to reveal His heart and the message that He desires to speak through you.

Now is the time for the Church to rise up in the power Jesus said where nothing will be impossible to us through prayer and fasting.

How hungry are you for more of God? The more you set yourself apart to seek His face through fasting and prayer, the more He will reveal Himself to you. And, the more you wait before Him, the more you will be changed into His image. Paul said, *"But we all, with open face beholding as in a glass the glory of the Lord, are changed into the same image from glory to glory, even as by the Spirit of the Lord" (2 Corinthians 3:18).*

It's Time To Pick Up Your Mighty Spiritual Weapons of Prayer amd Fasting!

We are living in a time of great turmoil and perplexity such as the world has never known. There are problems and circumstances we face in our personal lives as well as in our cities and nations for which there are no natural remedies.

Judgment upon the earth is coming. It will happen as it has been prophesied. But, God has placed within our hands the mighty weapons of fasting and prayer that are capable of moving His hand. As we pick up these mighty spiritual weapons, the Church of the living God can turn entire nations around as we prepare for the Day of the Lord.

God is not interested today in prayer and fasting "events" where people are mobilized to fast and pray for a specified period of time and then after the event is over, it is forgotten. Don't misunderstand what I am saying. I am not suggesting that pastors and Christian leaders shouldn't call and lead the Church in periodic fasts as God directs. However, the type of prayer and fasting I believe God is calling us to in this crucial hour is much more than just an occasional event or simple emphasis on prayer and fasting. We cannot continue just going through the motions or doing business as usual in the Church.

Jesus taught and demonstrated that through prayer and fasting we are able to walk in a dimension of power and anointing of the Holy Spirit where nothing shall be impossible to us! (Matthew 17:20-21) We can clearly see the great manifestation of the power of God that was released within the disciples in the Early Church, as they dedicated and consecrated themselves to God through fasting and prayer.

Now, it is time for the Church of the living God to rise up in the fullness of that power as we respond to this end-time call to fasting and prayer.

Through prayer and fasting we are able to penetrate into the realm of the spirit; engage Satan, his principalities, powers and the rulers of the darkness of this world and tear down the strongholds he has built in our lives, in the lives of others and throughout the nations of the world.

We must shake ourselves out of our complacency, hear the call of God's Spirit and rise up as a mighty army to fast, pray and wage spiritual warfare to move the hand of Almighty God on behalf of our families, cities and nations!

These powerful spiritual weapons of fasting and prayer are the means whereby you must engage the powers of darkness in your city and nation, defeat them and set the captives free!   He has given you these weapons to accomplish His purposes:

- To release His power to work on your behalf.

- To deliver you out of the hands of your enemies.

- To reveal His will to you.

- To provide for all your needs.

- To strengthen you in times of trouble.

- To empower you for service.

- To use you to wage war in the heavenlies on behalf of your family, city and nation.

Waging War In The Heavenlies

The great spiritual warrior Daniel stayed before the Lord in prayer and fasting 21 days before He received the answer he was seeking. As he humbled himself through prayer and fasting, it moved the hand of Almighty God!

On the 21st day something supernatural happened! An angelic being—a warrior angel—stood before him and said, "...Fear not, Daniel, for from the first day that you set your mind and heart to understand and to humble yourself before your God, your words were heard, and I have come in consequence of your words" (Daniel 10:12, AMP). When we begin to fast and pray according to God's purposes, something supernatural happens! Heaven responds!

Just as God heard Daniel on the very first day of his fast and dispatched an angel with the answer, He hears us. Our Father is not reluctant in answering our prayers. He is ready the moment we call to answer us. He has promised,

"Call unto me, and I will answer thee…" (Jeremiah 33:3), *and in Isaiah 65:24 "And it shall come to pass, that before* *they call I will answer; and while they are yet speaking, I* *will hear."*

On his way to Daniel, the angel was met with resistance by enemy forces. Look at verse 13: *"…But the prince of the kingdom of Persia withstood me for twenty-one days."* The angel was not referring to an earthly prince. The prince of Persia was one of the rulers of darkness and evil principalities that had been sent to stop him.

For twenty-one days, while Daniel was fighting this great battle in prayer and fasting, there was an intense battle going on in the spiritual realm. The angel God had dispatched with the answer was wrestling and fighting the evil ruler of darkness—the prince of Persia. Michael, God's mighty warrior angel, joined the combat and the angel was able to break through with the answer and revelation Daniel was seeking.

Daniel's fasting and prayer moved the hand of God. God honored his prayer and fasting. He spoke to Cyrus, a heathen king, to build Him a house in Jerusalem. Cyrus issued a proclamation stating that God had directed him to build him a house in Jerusalem, that all the Jews were free to return to Jerusalem to build the Temple, and that the people of the land were to assist them by giving silver and gold, goods and cattle and freewill offerings for the house of God! (Ezra 1:1-4).

Fasting And Prayer Breaks Through Demonic Resistance

Daniel set his mind to know the meaning of the vision he had received and was willing to stay on his face before God in fasting and prayer until he had received the revelation from God.

On the twenty-first day of Daniel's fast, when the angel broke through the demonic line of resistance, he came to Daniel and strengthened him. He said, "...*O man greatly beloved, fear not; peace be to you, be strong, yes, be strong...*" *(Daniel 10:19, AMP).* Then the angel revealed the meaning of the vision to him.

> On the 21st day of Daniel's fast something supernatural happened!

The important truth I want you to see in this example is that it was through prayer and fasting Daniel penetrated into the spirit realm, moved the hand of God and received the revelation he needed. In your life there will be times when you face battles where evil forces, powers and principalities have built strongholds in the lives of your loved ones and they are bound by drugs, alcohol or other addictions.

There will be times when you face problems in your family or in your finances where there seems to be no possible solution—where it seems you just cannot get an answer to your prayers.

There will be times when there are problems that are so overwhelming that you just don't know what to do and you must hear from God.

Fasting strengthens and intensifies your prayers. There will be times when, even after spending days in prayer, it will seem as if the heavens are brass and that you haven't been able to break through and receive the answer you need. But, as you begin to use your mighty weapons of prayer and fasting, you will be able to break through and claim victory.

The only way you will be able to break through the barrier and tear down those strongholds is to get on your face before God in times of prayer and fasting and stay there until you know satan's power is broken and you have the answer you need.

As You Fast and Pray, the Hosts of Heaven Join You

This example in Daniel's life reveals to us the warfare that takes place in the spirit that we are unable to see with our natural eyes.

The moment you begin to fast and pray, the Hosts of Heaven join with you!

> Fasting and prayer enables you to penetrate the spirit realm, break through the enemy's resistance and receive what you need from God.

In the battles you are fighting right now in your life, you are not fighting alone. The Hosts of Heaven are fighting with you. The Almighty God Jehovah is fighting for you! The promise Moses gave the children of Israel belongs to you: *"The Lord your God who*

goes before you will Himself fight on your behalf..."
(Deuteronomy 1:30, NAS).

The angels are fighting for you! *"The angel of the LORD encamps around those who fear him, and delivers them" (Psalm 34:7, NIV).* When Elisha was surrounded by the Syrian armies, he told his servant, *"...Do not fear, for those who are with us are more than those who are with them" (2 Kings 6:16, NAS).* Elisha saw into the spirit realm the angelic hosts of Heaven ready to fight on their behalf. Then God opened the eyes of Elisha's servant and allowed him to see that the mountain was full of a heavenly host, *"...horses and chariots of fire round about Elisha (2 Kings 6:17)*

The Holy Spirit intercedes for you! As you begin to pray, *"...the Spirit Himself goes to meet our supplication and pleads in our behalf with unspeakable yearnings and groanings too deep for utterance" (Romans 8:26, AMP).*

The Lord, Jesus Christ is praying for you! While He was on earth, Jesus prayed for His disciples. He told Peter, *"But I have prayed for thee, that thy faith fail not..." (Luke 22:32).* In John 17, we read His great high-priestly prayer that He prayed for all believers (John 17:20-21); and He is now at the right hand of the Father where He is making intercession for you! (Romans 8:34, Hebrews 7:25).

Where are the Ezra's and Esthers?

The power that the Church of Jesus Christ needs today—to tear down satan's strongholds, loose the bonds of sin, heal the sick, and set the captives free—can only be received on our knees, before God through fasting and prayer.

Today God is looking for men and women—like Moses, Daniel, Ezra, and Esther—who will fast, weep, mourn and stand in the gap for their homes, cities and nations. He is looking for those who will *"sigh and groan over all the abominations which are being committed in its midst" (Ezekiel 9:4, NAS).*

Are you ready to respond to His call today to make a new commitment to fasting and prayer and to live a lifestyle of fasting and prayer?

Perhaps the greatest example of how an entire city was spared because the people fasted and turned their hearts back to God is the story of Jonah and Ninevah. I briefly mentioned Ninevah in chapter three but I want you to realize that what God did for Ninevah in response to their prayer and fasting, He will do for any city or nation who will humble themselves and turn to Him.

God's ways are just and perfect. When He pronounces judgment upon a people or a nation, He has promised: *"If at any time I declare concerning a nation or a kingdom, that I will pluck up and break down and destroy it, and if that nation, concerning which I have spoken, turns from its evil, I will repent of the evil that I intended to do to it" (Jeremiah 18:7-8, RSV).*

God Saw Their Works and Spared Ninevah

God had pronounced judgment upon Ninevah and Jonah, God's man for the hour, was sent to warn them. Jonah cried, *"Yet forty days, and Ninevah shall be overthrown!" (Jonah 3:4).*

The city of Ninevah was facing imminent destruction. However, you will notice that they did not call the city council and their armies together to reason among themselves and to plan a strategy to save the city. Although they were living in such sin and degradation that their wickedness had come up before God, they did not turn to carnal weapons. Nor did they try to justify their evil ways. Look at verse 5: *"So the people of Ninevah believed God, and proclaimed a fast..."* The people believed God and the word spoken through His prophet and turned to Him in fasting and in mourning for their sins.

The king of Ninevah heard the warning from the prophet of God, believed it and humbled himself before God. He got up off his throne, took off his kingly robe, clothed himself in sackcloth and sat in ashes. Then he issued a decree proclaiming a total fast throughout the land that neither man nor beast could eat or drink. He said, *"Let neither man nor beast, herd nor flock, taste any thing: let them not feed, nor drink water; but let man and beast be covered with sackcloth, and cry mightily unto God; yea, let them turn every one from his evil way, and from the violence that is in their hands" (Jonah 3:7-8).*

The people of Ninevah didn't just go through some

religious exercise. It wasn't just their outward observance of the fast or the abstention from food and from drinking water that saved them. The king directed them to cry out in repentance and turn from their evil ways. In true repentance and mourning they turned from their evil ways and, as a result God heard them, *"And God saw their works, that they turned from their evil way; and God repented of the evil, that he had said that he would do unto them; and he did it not" (Jonah 3:10).*

Now is the Time To Hear God's Call and Respond

Now is the time when we must hear His call to unite in seasons of prayer and fasting until we see our cities and nations transformed by His mighty power.

Look around you! If ever there was a time when God's people needed to fast, it is today! Jesus said, *"... when the bridegroom will be taken from them; then they will fast" (Matthew 9:15, NIV).*

America, along with many other nations, is hanging in the balance. When we look at the immorality, sin and gross wickedness that fills our land, can we honestly believe that we will not face God's judgment unless we repent and turn back to Him?

Where are those who are willing to come before Him, as Moses did, fasting and crying out day and night for Him to spare the children of Israel?

In this end time call to prayer and fasting, God is calling His Church to lead the way in calling America and the nations to repentance and to stand in the gap in intercession on their behalf. Using these mighty weapons of prayer and fasting we can be used by God to turn entire nations around as we prepare for the Day of the Lord, when Christ will return and judgment will come upon the earth.

It is not a matter of can we do it, but will we do it! God has anointed and empowered us to do it. Remember Jesus' promise, *"If ye have faith as a grain of mustard seed, ye shall say unto this mountain, Remove hence to yonder place; and it shall remove; and nothing shall be impossible to you. Howbeit, this kind goeth not out but by prayer and fasting" (Matthew 17:20-21).*

We must no longer sit back, waiting for God to

supernaturally sweep through our cities and nations and do the work for us. He has called, anointed and empowered the Church to reach our cities and nations in a mighty demonstration of His power.

He has given us the awesome responsibility and privilege through prayer and fasting to move His hand on behalf of our families, cities and nations.

Will You Answer the Call?

The time has come for the Church to unite as a powerful force to fast and pray to move God's hand on behalf of entire nations, such as Egypt, Tunisia, Libya, Sudan, Haiti and many others that are in crisis right now.

Answer God's call today and make fasting and prayer part of your lifestyle! God is calling us to fast and pray on behalf of unreached people groups with millions who have never heard the Gospel, break the yokes of bondage and proclaim salvation, healing and deliverance in Jesus' Name.

It is time for us to unite through strategic prayer and fasting to move God's hand to break down the walls of opposition in nations now closed to the Gospel and believe Him for new doors of freedom for the spreading of the Gospel.

I encourage every pastor and Christian leader to set aside specific periods of time throughout the year to fast and pray, and to call their churches to fast and pray, not only for the needs of the people in their churches, but also to fast in repentance and intercession on behalf of their cities and nations.

In addition to this universal end-time call to corporate prayer and fasting within the Church, He is raising up an army of men and women who will dedicate themselves to a lifestyle of fasting and prayer. Not only will these spiritual warriors participate in corporate calls to fasting and prayer, they will also set aside regular fast days each week to seek God on behalf of their personal needs, families, cities and nations.

If you have not already done so, my prayer is that you will answer this end-time call of the Spirit and make a commitment today before God to develop a lifestyle of fasting and prayer.

In your home, church, city, and nation, be the one who is willing to pay the price, the one who will fast and pray until you see God's power released!

Be the one whom God will use to spare your nation and to release spirits of salvation, healing and deliverance upon it! Be the one whom He will use to tear down Satan's strongholds and loose the captives!

WALKING IN THE SUPERNATURAL:

God has confirmed T.L. Lowery's ministry through powerful signs and wonders. These include complete healing of those who were...

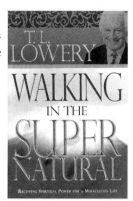

  *severely crippled
  *in an advanced stage of leprosy
  *demon possessed
  *totally deaf and mute
  *raised from the dead

Discover how you can personally receive God's healing touch and how God can use you to bring His love and healing to others. Christ's transforming power and grace will change your life from ordinary to extraordinary.

PASSING THE TORCH DVDs
TITANIUM COLLECTION

This is the collection of the 3 main events for the 2010 Passing The Torch Conferences. Be a part of the 3 major gatherings held in 3 key cities in 2010. These conferences created an environment for souls to be saved, individuals filled with the fire of the Holy Ghost and both of these were

realized. Feel the anointing that was experienced and hear the powerful Word revealed at these special events. Ministries such as: TL Lowery, Tommy Bates, Rod Parsley, Mike Brown, Mark Casto, Donna Lowry, Perry Stone & Eddie James. The torch of the Holy Spirit will be passed to every generation that will seek the Father for an uncommon move of God...Don't miss this! Are you ready to be ignited with fresh fire?!

To order, please call: 423.473.4562 or Toll Free: 866.473.4676
www.tllowery.org

ONE YEAR BIBLICAL STUDY – OLD TESTAMENT & NEW TESTAMENTS

The Bible is the measuring rod for understanding what we believe and how we are to live. Yet all too often, the Holy Scriptures are a mystery to us. All of us would like to familiarize ourselves with the Word of God but do not know where to start. The One Year Biblical Study material is a tool that will  benefit any Christian in comprehending the whole counsel of God contained in the Scriptures. The complete set, Old and New Testament, contains fifty-two easy, concise lessons. There are two resource components: the teaching manuscript and the lesson outline. It has been designed to guide you through the entire Bible in one year's time. Some churches have dedicated their Sunday School Class or weeknight services to this study. This material is so flexible that individuals can utilize it for self-study.

APOSTLES & PROPHETS

God is restoring divine order to the body of Christ. He is preparing the church for a greater outpouring of the Holy Spirit than we have ever experienced. A questioning world longs to know for sure what the Bible teaches about the purpose, identity and function of apostles and prophets. As the original twelve laid the foundation for the development of the people of God and the establishment of the church, today's apostles and prophets perform foundational ministry for the continuing building of the church. This Scriptural work is undergirded with unimpeachable sources and verifiable evidences.

To order, please call: 423.473.4562 or Toll Free: 866.473.4676
www.tllowery.org

NOTES:

Chapter One:

1. Wesley, John. "Upon Our Lord's Sermon on the Mount, VII". Sermon 27. In The Works of John Wesley, Volume I. Edited by Albert C. Outler. Nashville: Abington Press, 1984

1. Proclamation for a day of Fasting and Prayer, June 12, 1775.

2. John Adams, "A Proclamation," March 23, 1978; printed in the Philadelphia Weekly Magazine, March 31, 1798.

3. Expanded from the version sent by the U.S. Senate: Journal of the Senate, March 2, 1863 A Century of Lawmaking for a New Nation: U.S. Congressional Documents and Debates, 1774-1875, The Library of Congress.

4. Abraham Lincoln Online – Proclamation Appointing a National Fast Day.

Chapter Two:

1. Franklin Hall, Atomic Power with God, Franklin Hall Ministries, 1947.

2. Jason Mandryk, Operation World professional edition DVD-ROM, (Colorado Srings, CO, Biblica Publishing, 2010) p. 25.

3. Derek Prince, Shaping History Through Prayer and Fasting, (New Kensington, PA, Whitaker House, 2002), pages 71-75.

4. Andrew Murray, Andrew Murray on Prayer-With Christ in

the School of Prayer, (New Kensington, PA, Whitaker House, 1998).

Chapter Three:

1. Andrew Murray, Andrew Murray on Prayer-With Christ in the School of Prayer, (New Kensington, PA, Whitaker House, 1998)p. 373.

2. Jentezen Franklin, Fasting (Lake Mary, FL, Charisma House, 2008), pages 9-10

3. Mahesh Chavda, The Hidden Power of Prayer & Fasting, (Shippensburg, PA, Destiny Image Publishers, Inc, 1998) p. 82.

Chapter Four:

1. Gordon Cove, Revival Now Through Prayer & Fasting, (Nicholasville, KY, Schmul Publishing Company).

2. Jentezen Franklin, Fasting (Lake Mary, FL, Charisma House, 2008), pages 101-102.

Chapter Five:

1. Bob Rodgers, The 21 Day Fast (Louisville, KY, Bob Rodgers Ministries, 2001), pages 92-93.

2. Bob Rodgers, The 21 Day Fast (Louisville, KY, Bob Rodgers Ministries, 2001), pages 8-9, 63.

3. Jentezen Franklin, Fasting (Lake Mary, FL, Charisma House, 2008), pages 99-100.

Chapter Six:

1. Rodgers, 101 Reasons to Fast, p. 53

2. Mahesh Chavda, The Hidden Power of Prayer & Fasting, (Shippensburg, PA, Destiny Image Publishers, Inc, 1998) p. 173.